LAST DAY ON EARTH

LAST DAY ON EARTH

A PORTRAIT OF THE NIU SCHOOL SHOOTER

DAVID VANN

THE UNIVERSITY OF GEORGIA PRESS

ATHENS

This is a work of creative nonfiction. It draws from primary source
materials including police files and other documents, as well as many
hours of interviews. The author has made every effort to reconstruct
dialog, scenes, descriptions, and motivations as accurately as possible.
Names and identifying characteristics of some persons have
been changed to protect their privacy.

Published by the University of Georgia Press
Athens, Georgia 30602
www.ugapress.org
© 2011 by David Vann
All rights reserved
Set in Scala
Printed and bound by Sheridan Books
The paper in this book meets the guidelines for
permanence and durability of the Committee on
Production Guidelines for Book Longevity of the
Council on Library Resources.

Printed in the United States of America

11   12   13   14   15   C   5   4   3   2   1

Library of Congress Cataloging-in-Publication Data
Vann, David.
    Last day on earth : a portrait of the NIU school shooter / David Vann.
        p. cm. — (Association of writers and writing programs award for
creative nonfiction)
    ISBN 978-0-8203-3839-2 (cloth : alk. paper)
    1. Kazmierczak, Steve. 2. Mass murder—Illinois—De Kalb.
3. Youth and violence—Illinois—De Kalb. 4. School shootings—
Illinois—De Kalb. 5. Campus violence—Illinois—De Kalb.
6. Northern Illinois University—Students. I. Title.
    HV6534.D434V36 2011
    364.152'34092—dc23

2011018019

Parts of this book originally appeared in *Esquire, Men's Journal, Esquire UK,*
and the *Sunday Telegraph.*

Nothing human is foreign to me.

TERENCE
(195–159 BC)

I tried to peer around the podium to get a look at him, but the
minute I saw him, he turned and saw me. He turned and fired,
and he pulled the trigger of the Glock multiple times. He just kept
shooting me. I got hit right in the head. It felt like getting hit with
a bat. As I fell to the floor face first, all I could think was,
"I got shot and I'm dead." I hit the floor with my eyes closed and
a ringing sound in my ear, and I thought this was literally the
sound of my dying, going into the darkness.

BRIAN KARPES,
survivor of the NIU school shooting,
February 14, 2008

LAST DAY ON EARTH

AFTER MY FATHER'S SUICIDE, I inherited all his guns. I was thirteen. Late at night, I reached behind my mother's coats in the hall closet for the barrel of my father's .300 magnum rifle. It was cold and heavy, smelled of gun oil. I carried it down the hallway, through kitchen and pantry into the garage, where I turned on the light and gazed at it, a bear rifle with a scope, bought in Alaska for grizzlies. The world had been emptied, but this gun had a presence still, an undeniable power. My father had used it on deer. It sounded like artillery, would tear the entire shoulder off a deer hundreds of yards away. I pulled back the bolt, sighted in on a cardboard box across the garage. A box of track for an electric train, and one small rail sticking up filled the scope. I held my breath as my father had taught, squeezed carefully, slowly, heard a metallic click.

With a screwdriver, I separated stock from barrel. I put both pieces down the back of my jacket, cinched under my belt. They stuck out from my collar behind my head but were mostly hidden. I wheeled my bicycle, an old Schwinn Varsity ten-speed, out the back door and through a gate in our fence.

Our neighborhood was silent at 3:00 a.m. Cold still in early April, 1980, a light mist in the air. I huffed up a steep hill in low gear, hot in my father's jacket, starting to sweat by the time I hit the top. Then coasted down the other side, my ears cold. Big houses, trim lawns, but several streetlights knocked out. Broken somehow, a few remaining shards of glass on the pavement below.

Up the next hill, I pulled off to the side, an undeveloped lot, tall grass and a few oak trees. I hid my bicycle behind one of them and hiked away from the houses until finally I hit a small clearing and had a view. Much of Hidden Valley, in Santa Rosa, California, lay before me.

The rifle went together quickly, and I pulled three shells from my pocket. So much powder packed into the brass. Magnum means too much powder, a bullet sent at much higher speed. I pushed all three shells into the magazine, pulled back the bolt, clicked off the safety. Sat back against the hillside with my feet planted wide, elbows on my knees, forming a base.

Through the scope, I traced houses. Went along their bedroom windows, held crosshairs on their front doors, on taillights of cars in their driveways. Finally zeroed in on a streetlight, rounded and smooth and bright, large in the scope. I could see the bulb inside. Never closer than 100 yards, most of the time two or three times that far, and most of the time, I didn't pull the trigger. It was enough simply to imagine. But sometimes that wasn't enough. Sometimes I wanted more. On those nights, I felt the blood in my temples, a pounding my father had called buck fever when we hunted deer, my breath gone, my heart become hard as a fist. I tried to steady, squeezed slowly, and felt afraid of the shock to come.

When I fired, the rifle kicked so hard it sometimes blew me flat on my back. I'd had a .30-.30 since I was nine, was used to rifles, but the .300 magnum was outrageous. If I was lucky, I'd hit my target and also stay upright. Nothing was more beautiful to me than the blue-white explosion of a streetlight seen through crosshairs. The sound of it—the pop that was almost a roar, then silence, then glass rain—came only after each fragment and shard had sailed off or twisted glittering in the air like mist.

Dogs would bark, lights come on. And if anyone in my field of view parted their curtains to look out, I pulled back the bolt to put a new shell in the chamber, sighted in. A man's face, centered in the crosshairs, lit from his bedside lamp, the safety off and my finger held to the side, just above the trigger. I had done this with my father. When he spotted poachers—hunters trespassing on our land—he would have me look at them through the scope.

These were not my darkest moments that year. I imagined many things, even shooting my classmates at school. I lived a double life. A straight-A student who would become valedictorian. In student government, band, sports, etc. No one would have guessed.

So when I read about Steve Kazmierczak, a Deans' Award winner who killed five students and himself at Northern Illinois University on Valentine's Day 2008 and wounded eighteen others, I wondered. He was an A student. His friends and professors couldn't make any sense of what had happened. This wasn't the Steve they knew. I had never been interested in mass murderers before and couldn't have imagined reading a book about one, much less writing one, but I wondered whether Steve might offer a view into why it is that sometimes the worst part of us wins out. Why had I not ended up hurting anyone? How had I escaped, and why hadn't he?

As I investigated Steve for *Esquire*, as I gained access to the full fifteen-hundred-page police file that had been withheld from all others—from the *New York Times*, *Chicago Tribune*, *Washington Post*, CNN—I found the story of someone who really did almost escape, who almost managed to avoid becoming a mass murderer, someone trying to make something of himself after a wretched childhood and mental health history, someone attempting the American Dream, which is not only about money but about the remaking of self. His life had been far more terrible than mine, his successes a far greater triumph, but through him I could understand, finally, the most frightening moments of my own life and also what I find most frightening about America.

STEVE GREW UP WATCHING HORROR MOVIES with his mother. Fleshy, enormous, laid out beside him on the couch. Middle of the day, and all shades are drawn. Dark. She's protective, doesn't want Steve to go outside. Won't let him play much with other children. She's not mentally right, according to Steve's godfather, but what can he do? A family feud.

Horror movies and the Bible, those are what animate this living room, those are Steve's inheritance. A close fit, the plagues, the tortures of Job. God's sadistic games, teaching his flock to appreciate the value and meaning of their lives. The flesh of no consequence. Late night, his mother can't sleep. An insomniac with anxiety problems. His father playing out a family history of depression, Steve's grandfather an alcoholic. So they continue on, still watching.

At school, Steve is an average student. "Steve appears very impulsive and does not want to go back and check his work, therefore there are a lot of errors. At our conference we can discuss ways to help Steve work up to his potential," writes his third-grade teacher, Ms. Moser. A few years later, Iowa test score fifty-eighth percentile. By now he's looking for places to hide, tries to find something like the living room, finds it at last in the band practice rooms of Grove Junior High. Plays tenor sax, has a friend, Adam Holzer, skinny and geeky with a nervous smile and round glasses far too large for his face. Long straight hair hanging slack, parted in the middle. Steve no looker himself. Face too skinny at the bottom, almost no mouth or chin, and whenever he focuses on work, he forgets himself. The back of his wrist against his forehead, hand hanging out limply. His mouth open, a piece of food always caught in a gap between his lower front teeth. Other kids call him fag because of the hand. He and Adam get notes to leave class as often as possible, especially gym class, whenever a concert or performance of any kind is on the schedule. One of the rooms is small and has no windows. Here they can talk, eat candy, hide away.

After school, they go home to Steve's, 758 Penrith, Elk Grove Village, Illinois. A small tract home, one story, three small bedrooms. If it weren't for the living room extending a few extra feet, the house would be a perfect rectangle, same as a double-wide. His mother is a secretary, his father a letter carrier. They won't be home for hours.

A bedroom community, four variations on this tract house, and Steve's butts up against a major road, four lanes. Only a chain-link fence between the small back lawn and the cars.

Steve goes straight for the pellet gun, walks outside to the shed, perfect cover. He pumps the gun, building up air pressure, slides in a small pellet, and closes the bolt.

He can hear his dog breathing, though, up close. A pug with breathing problems. So he picks it up by its hind legs and hurls it, hard, with both hands, against the wall.

Now he can focus. The cars are going fast, and they're only in view for a couple car lengths. And the pellet is slow. So he has to hold the gun aimed to the right, and the moment a car flashes in from the left, he pulls the trigger. The gun spits, the sound of air released, and then he and Adam hang for a moment in concentration, in hope, waiting for the sound of a pellet hitting metal.

They squeal if they hear it, their joy as compressed as the air in the gun. Wait and watch as drivers try to come back, try to pinpoint them. Not easy to do on a busy, fast-moving street. A few times, drivers circle around through the neighborhood, even figure out the right house. The doorbell or loud knocking, but the door is locked, the lights out. The joy so complete, it's nearly impossible to keep quiet.

Even better than the pellet gun, though, is Pete Rachowsky. A kid in Steve's grade who carries the materials for a Drano bomb in his backpack. Plastic bottle, Drano or Works toilet cleaner, aluminum foil. Simple. He teaches more than a dozen kids how to make the bombs. Steve and one of his few friends, Joe Russo, decide to make one. Maybe it's a way to cement the friendship with Joe. Steve is very protective of his friends, realizes there aren't many who will have him.

They wait until after dinner on February 5, 1994. A Saturday night, eighth grade. Joe meets him at the corner and they walk to Jewel supermarket, only a couple blocks away. Steve has a two-liter plastic bottle in his backpack. They buy Works toilet cleaner and aluminum foil, worry about getting caught. Steve comes in here all the time with Adam to eat candy out of the bulk bins. He's used to feeling nervous here. He's ready to say his mother asked him to buy these things, but the checker doesn't ask.

They walk along Arlington Heights, the busy street behind Steve's house. They take a left on Cosman and walk the strip of houses that face the forest preserve. At the corner, they pass the barn and cottage of the preserve and keep going. This is the way to Joe's house, so they can say they're just going home. The houses here look across the street at a hundred feet of lawn and then trees. Easy to disappear anywhere along here, and there's not much traffic.

They find a house that's dark, no one home, no cars in the driveway. 235 Cosman, a two-story with an indented porch. They sneak up to this porch, tiptoeing, and crouch down. Steve pulls out the bottle, and they stuff aluminum foil into it. A lot of foil, and then Steve worries it's too much, but they pour in the Works, cap it, and run across the street to hide in the trees.

Nothing happens for a while. They wonder if they made it wrong. They think about running back across to check. Then it blows, an explosion louder than they could have hoped for. Glorious. They run back through the forest, hyped up on adrenaline and joy, laughing.

Five days later, on February 10, Pete's mother, MaryAnn Rachowsky, finds two-liter bottles, Works toilet cleaner, and aluminum foil in her son's backpack. She tells the police, they haul Pete in for questioning, and he eventually gives up Steve and Joe.

The detectives call Steve's parents on the twenty-second, and they agree to bring him in for questioning. "We spoke to Steven's parents and they related that Steven was very nervous and scared about being at the police station and he realized that what he had done was a mistake," reads the police report from February 24, 1994. "They advised that they would discipline him and would like us to speak to Steven to scare him in order that he would not make any bombs in the future."

Steve is remorseful. He tells the police that fifteen students know how to make the bombs. He gives names. He vows he'll never do something like this again. Does he already hate himself at this point? Are his apologies already over the top, as they will be in later years? The police aren't psychiatrists and of course can't see the future. They see only a scared, remorseful kid, a minor offense, no property damage, no injuries. They station-adjust him, close the case, send him home to be disciplined by his parents.

MY OWN JUVENILE REPORT IS FROM 1980. Only one contact with the Santa Rosa police, and not with the .300 magnum. It was a BB gun, a hot summer's day, at the fence in our backyard. A fifteen-foot drop-off to the neighbors' yard below, since we were on a hill. Pine trees along the fence, shady and hidden. My mother at work.

I usually shot at birds with the BB gun and also a pellet gun, but today the neighbors' dog was barking at me. A black Lab, like the one I'd had with my father. I'd spent weekends at his ranch in Lakeport, California, before he moved back to Alaska. That dog had greeted me every Friday evening by knocking me flat. I'd see the white diamond on his chest, then I'd hit the ground.

I don't know why I decided to shoot at the neighbors' dog. I have only the facts of Steve's life to understand what he did, the details of scenes, and really that's all I have from my own life. I can't remember enough of what I felt or thought twenty-eight years ago. A self is not a constant thing, and a mind changes from year to year and can't remember how it thought before. We think we remember, but that's fiction, built on the few facts that were noted and stored away.

A beautiful dog, rich black coat, tail wagging as it barked. It was on a back porch that was only a concrete slab in front of a sliding glass door to the living room. The neighbors' yard was large, with a lot of trees, so the dog was at least fifty feet away, maybe more, and I do remember thinking that a BB was far too slow to do any damage, especially at this range. At the most, it would feel like a swat.

I aimed a couple feet above the dog's back to account for the fall of the BB and pulled the trigger. A light cough of air, and the brass BB arced away and fell even lower than I had thought, hitting the concrete under the dog's belly and slapping into the sliding glass door behind. Then there was a pause. The dog wasn't barking. I wasn't breathing, and all was still. I could see the BB stuck in the glass, but since that was impossible, I thought I was imagining it.

The glass moved in waves. Large ripples over its entire length, become a liquid, something I had never seen, something I didn't know was possible, and then it exploded. The entire sliding glass door shattered into thousands of fragments.

The sound was loud, and I should have been running away, but I had just witnessed the most beautiful and improbable thing.

Then the neighbors' sons emerged from the shattered doorway and I ducked down. They were yelling, and after a few more moments, I heard them start up their VW van and roar down their street to come around the block.

I ran into the house with the BB gun, to the hallway closet, pushed it behind my mother's coats and pulled out my old BB gun, the broken one. I ran back outside to our shed and was opening the door when I happened to see my neighbor, Ned, looking out his bedroom window at me. He was a year or two younger than I was, a small kid, and we were friends, sort of. I had shot him once with the BB gun, a really lucky shot as he ran down the sidewalk away from me. Just pointed the gun high in the air, and he was far away, running fast, but the BB somehow arced perfectly and hit him in the back. Luckiest shot of my life, and today had been the unluckiest.

I put my finger to my lips to ask Ned to keep this a secret, then ducked into the shed to place the BB gun and ran back inside the house.

The van pulled up, the neighbors pounding at our front door. Did I open the door and talk with them? I remember their yelling, and I remember what they looked like, two older boys in high school, stoners with long hair, and I remember feeling frightened, but I could have been watching through the peephole.

When my mother came home, she believed in my innocence. She wanted to clear my good name. So we drove around to the neighbors and sat in their living room next to that shattered, missing door, and she laid into them for how their sons had frightened me. She was a school counselor, an authority of sorts. But they knew I had shot at their dog, which pissed them off even more than the glass.

My mother then took me to Ned's house. I remember sitting down with Ned's parents. Ned had squealed on me already about hiding the BB gun, but his father said something like "we know David's a good boy," and Ned's mother pursed her lips and made it clear she knew that wasn't true. My mother looked at me then, a curious look, as if I were some new kind of monster.

Then we visited our other neighbors. They reported seeing me on the roof with a pellet gun, said they were tired of me shooting all the doves off the telephone wires. They liked doves, and no doves came here anymore.

My mother called the police. I was still maintaining my innocence, and she wanted the truth. I thought it was bad form, personally, to call the police on your own son, but she cared only about truth and justice, not distracted at all by blood.

I lucked out, though. The cop who arrived was the daughter of "Green," our neighbor at our previous house, an older woman who became like a grandmother to me and my sister.

The three of us stood at the fence right where I had stood to fire the shot. "Can you trace the angle the BB was shot from, some sort of ballistics?" my mother asked. She seemed ready to pay for the test herself.

"It must have come from up the hill," I said.

We went into the shed to look at the BB gun. "It's broken," I said. "It doesn't even work. I thought about trying to hide it because I was scared, but then Ned saw me, so I just put it back."

Green's daughter tested the gun, and it was indeed broken. My mother didn't know about the other BB gun. But she told Green's daughter about my pellet gun stunts and everything we'd learned from the neighbors.

Green's daughter thought for a while, then said I was a good kid, I got good grades, I shouldn't be shooting BB guns or pellet guns, but we'd never know what happened to that sliding glass door. It wasn't possible to figure out the angle of fire with a BB. She said we should just assume I was innocent and let it go.

So nothing happened, and I continued shooting. From *Survivalist Magazine* I ordered a converter kit for the .300 magnum that allowed me to shoot .32-caliber pistol shells in the rifle. They were much quieter and could be mistaken, even, for firecrackers. They were very accurate through that long barrel, and I could hit streetlights right from my own backyard.

I ordered the converter kit with my mother's knowledge and blessing. This was the time of nuclear holocaust fears, of *The Day After* and *The Beach*, and she liked the idea of squirreling away some food and water. We had long excited talks about how I would be able to hunt and provide for the family in times of Armageddon, and this converter kit was a part of that plan, would allow me to kill small game with a rifle that could also snipe bad guys with its full .300 magnum shells. These discussions put us very close to the Michigan Militia that Steve admired, put us dangerously close to his libertarianism, to the primacy of the individual or small clan over the larger group or society, especially the federal government. It was insanity, but it wasn't uncommon at the time.

I also tried, like Steve, to make bombs. I filled a small glass apple juice bottle with gasoline and stuffed a rag in the top, set it in the middle of a neighboring street late at night, and lit it on fire, then ran back a hundred feet. Nothing happened. I didn't know how a Molotov cocktail was supposed to work, didn't realize it had to be thrown and shattered, that it wasn't technically a bomb. I couldn't consult with anyone, because I had realized early on that if you want to commit crimes, you have to do them alone. No one else can be trusted.

I HAVE TO GO BACK TO STEVE'S DOG, the pug, because even though "nothing human is foreign to me," Steve does things early on that strain that idea.

Adam watches Steve drop the pug numerous times, light it on fire. Its loud breathing just really annoys the shit out of Steve. Then one of Steve's other friends, Joe Cuzma, comes to tap at his window. This is eighth grade, the same year as the Drano bomb, and they don't have cell phones yet. They just knock on each other's windows. But Joe looks in Steve's window and sees him behind his dog, fucking it. At least this is what he tells everyone at school. "That guy's messed up," he says. Joe is tall, excitable, his head waving around and tongue lolling as he holds an imaginary dog and air-fucks it. Everyone laughs. Everyone.

"I was teaching it dominance," Steve tells Adam and another friend, Rich Johnson. "I was showing it who was alpha dog." And this isn't the same as denying it happened.

Steve loses friends, Joe Cuzma and others. He's very protective of his remaining friends, worries that Adam is spending too much time with Joe Russo and Lee Bode, worries Adam will steal them away and he'll have no one. So he starts talking about Adam behind his back and doesn't know that Joe and Lee tell this to Adam.

Adam has another thing Steve wants, a new business with a friend Mike, raising feeder mice and rats for snakes. Steve wants in. So Adam invites him over, a setup. "I arranged a wiretap," Adam says. He hides a tape recorder, and when Steve arrives, they talk. Steve's looking at the tanks, figuring his way in, mice scrabbling at the glass, the smell of sawdust and urine. Adam leads with questions to get Steve to admit he doesn't like certain people, gets him to say bad things about them. Steve's barely even paying attention, worried about what he has to offer, how he can become a part of this. Adam gets him to admit he stole CD's and liquor from Joe Russo's older brother and sister.

Later that week, on Friday afternoon, Steve goes over to Joe Russo's house, another tract home like his own, but right across from the preserve, away from traffic, on a corner with a larger lawn. Joe, Lee, and Adam are playing a video game on the TV, and this is what Steve fears, Adam taking away his best friends. He tries not to say anything, because Joe's dad is in the other room. He sits down and then Adam turns off the game. He hits play on a tape recorder, and there it is, for all to hear. What Steve has said about his friends, his admission that he stole from Joe's sister and brother. He tries to stop it, tries to get to the tape recorder, but Adam stops him, and then Steve starts hitting Adam, screaming.

"He lost all his friends that day," Adam says.

The next day, Steve challenges Adam to a fight after school. Other kids hear about it. Steve pulls a knife.

"It's not worth it," Adam tells him, scared shitless. "All these people, everyone will see. You'll get in trouble."

And Steve sees this is true, sees that Adam has cornered him yet again. Then he gets suspended, and Adam only gets detention.

Joe Russo's older brother is on the football team. He tells all his buddies Steve is bad news, and word gets around. When Steve enters high school as a ninth-grader in the fall, he's already an outcast.

Goths. This is what Steve and his friends become in high school, except that Steve is an outcast even within this group. Just beyond the school grounds is a parking lot where they all gather and smoke. Long black trench coats, black leather boots, chains and spikes. Officer Lancaster lurking at the edges with his bionic mic, trying to catch drug deals.

It takes time, unbearable time, all of ninth grade and into tenth grade, for Steve to regain his friendships with Joe and Lee, and there's always an edge with Adam. Steve waits for his life to change, passes the time with Pete Rachowsky, who becomes a drug dealer.

Steve and his friends form a campus club in the fall of their sophomore year, try to get a radio station. It starts with just a few short bits to go with campus announcements a couple times a day. Free Your Minds, they call the club, and it's unsuccessful. They're not liked, after all. Who would want to listen to them?

Steve doesn't care much, though. Somehow, the miraculous has happened. A girl named "Missy" likes him for some reason, and suddenly he has a girlfriend. She's cute, too, looks like Liv Tyler, wears a black choker. His parents let her stay over a couple nights a week as a "family friend." Then, in the winter, Missy dumps him, tells everyone he has a small penis, can't satisfy her in bed. Steve's older sister, Susan, is no help. She laughs at him too. She's always had an easier time. The two of them are night and day.

So Steve goes for the lowest common denominator, "Nicole," "a girl with a self-esteem problem, a girl you wouldn't want your parents to know about," according to Adam. Secret sex for that entire summer after tenth grade. No one is supposed to know, except Steve's friends. At Rich's house, there's a foam lounger that reclines. They call it the Flip-N-Fuck. They do it on the ottoman, too, in Rich's living room late at night, just a moving sheet with two bodies underneath.

I COMMITTED MY CRIMES ALONE partly because, like Steve, I was losing all my friends. Eighth grade was the time of "cut-downs," competitive insults. After my father's death, I was weak. Ian VanTuyl, who had been my best friend, began using everything he knew against me. At school, on the blacktop, we'd all stand around in a circle with our hands in our pockets and Ian would say that my front teeth were too big, or I smiled too much, and I would grin weakly and not know what to say. This is how you become a target in junior high. Others in the group were relieved, because this meant they were no longer targets, and they heaped it on. Every day I was made fun of, every day, all day, and so I know some of the rage Steve must have felt, and I know what it means to be an outcast in your social group.

Like Steve, I turned to secret sex. A girl with a terrible reputation, someone from a poorer part of town. At her house after school, her parents never home, we made out on her bed. I put my finger inside her and couldn't believe how soft she was, but then she said we could have sex, and this scared me too much. I wasn't ready. I had limits. My friends were just starting to drink, but I refused. It was something about control. My father's suicide had come as a shock, and perhaps I couldn't sleep and couldn't drink and couldn't have sex because I wasn't willing to let something happen again that would be beyond my control.

I broke up with this girl, and then a guy named Ryan started having sex with her and telling everyone about it at school, started calling me a pussy. So now my friends had two new ways to make fun of me, about drinking and about sex. I still invited them for sleepovers, and had an agreement with my mother that we could go out toilet-papering people's houses and such and she'd pretend not to notice. One time she forgot and came out into the hallway when she heard a sound, so then she had to shield her eyes, looking down, pretending she was really sleepy, as she talked to me and we all stood there with TP in our hands. She was a good actress.

Outside, toilet-papering a house, my friends still made fun of me, but I had an edge they didn't. I'd stick around as they all ran away. I'd walk up into the yard and unscrew the light bulb on the front porch, walk around into the backyard, even. Compared to what I was doing at night on my own, none of this felt like anything.

In the afternoons, I was going into neighbors' houses. I had their phone numbers, and this was right before answering machines became widespread, so I would simply call their house and let it ring the entire time I was inside. If anyone came home, they would rush for the phone and I would slip out the way I'd come in, which was always through the small sliding bathroom window. Everyone in our neighborhood left that window open. It was difficult to climb in, headfirst, balancing on the toilet and trying not to break anything, but it always worked.

I never stole anything. I think I was just alone, an outcast, with a life that felt empty, so I was looking at all the stuff of other peoples' lives, trying to see or feel what made them. I also looked for pornography, of course, and guns.

I had fantasies during this time that cast me as the underdog, everyone against me. I would imagine myself out behind the school backstop with the .30-.30 having to defend the honor of some girl as my classmates, all boys, attacked. I held them off, shooting them one by one with the rifle. So it was a fantasy born of reading too many of my father's westerns, Louis L'Amour and later the adults-only ones by Jake Slocum. It was the fantasy of an outcast becoming a hero, showing everyone. But there I was, imagining a school shooting.

STEVE SPENDS ALMOST NO TIME AT HOME. He lives at his friends' houses the fall of eleventh grade. He's better friends now with Julie Creamer, a big girl who's on lithium for bipolar, same as Steve. His parents put him on it. It helps a bit. You'd never know Julie was on it; she's light and fun and chatty. Her mother asks for help moving the furniture, and Steve handles it himself, tells her to relax, he'll take care of it. Home away from home. He feels safe here.

At school, in the parking lot where all the Goths hang out, Julie gets Steve to try pot for the first time. He's resisted before, even with Pete, but she gets him to try pot she's bought from Pete, and he's skipping around afterward, like a new bird. She's laughing and trying to get him to stop. "Lancaster will bust us," she tells him.

The other hangout is at The Tubes. A short walk to the forest preserve, hop a fence, slog though mud and wet grass past the federal nursery, rows of trees. In the next field, a dozen leftover concrete sewer pipes six feet in diameter, tall enough to stand inside. Shelter from rain and snow, the constant wind. He tries to get Julie to give him head here, but when they kiss, it's awkward. She feels like she's kissing her brother, and she wonders whether he's really attracted to her. They date for two days, then decide to just be friends.

Most the time, at least half a dozen of their friends are here. They light chemicals on fire, blow shit up, shoot pellet guns, make out, smoke pot, sneak away to the porno stash in the trees. Whenever they shoot, Steve brags he has a membership with the NRA. His godfather, Richard Grafer, bought it for him.

"We know," Adam says. "Like you haven't told us a million times." Adam and Steve are friends again, sort of, and they bring white spray paint one day for tagging. Steve tags a white swastika on the front of one of the pipes. "You're doing your swastika wrong," Adam says.

"No I'm not," Steve says.

"Remember how you used to put 'Hi Ho Hitler' instead of 'Heil Hitler'?"

"Shut up. I'll show you what's real." And Steve gives Adam a business card from the KKK. Then he tags "blows" under "Metallica," even though he loves Metallica.

On colder nights, they hang out in one of the bathrooms. Steve's godfather, Grafer, works for the forest service, for Cook County, so Steve has access to the keys. The bathrooms are cinderblock stand-alone huts in the wilderness. Their own concrete chalets. They're used, also, by gay cruisers. If you back into a parking space here, you're asking for a visit.

Steve has been with a man before, but his friends don't know this. Secret sex, like his summer with Nicole.

Steve hangs out a lot with Pete Rachowsky. They get arrested September 22, 1996, for trespassing on railroad tracks and the Pepsi lot, planning to go through some dumpsters. By the end of the semester, as it gets colder, Steve has become odd, even for him, and antisocial.

"Is something going on at home?" Julie asks him.

"Nothing," he says. "I don't want to talk about it."

Steve decides to commit suicide, plans it ahead of time, holds a sale first to get rid of all his stuff. His friend Jason gets his guitar. His friend Lee gets his video games. "He sold all his shit," Adam says.

December 14, 1996, Steve overdoses on Tylenol and calls Missy. His parents throw him into Rush, a hospital, for a week, but something becomes unstoppable about these suicide attempts. Steve is anxious all the time, depressed, unable to sleep. He blows up on the meds, goes from skinny to obese, 300 pounds, in just a couple months. Rich can't understand what's happened. Steve is like a zombie, with a faraway stare, "like the personality was just sucked out of him." Julie tries to talk with him, and most the time he's just glassy-eyed, so out of it he won't even look at her.

In one clear moment, he stands at the mirror with her, at her house. He has terrible acne, one of the side effects. "You don't need makeup," he tells her. "You look beautiful. I look like shit. Look at me. This is horrible."

People talk about him at school that winter. He's sitting in the cafeteria, an enormous and exposed room right off the main hall, a place where you can't hide. He's with Julie, and a couple of jocks come up to him. They know his sister, Susan, and they know Joe Russo's older brother and sister. They know everything about him. "Hey, Suicide Steve, what's up?" one of them asks. "Uh-oh, don't say that, Crazy Mierczak might off himself," the other says. Then the first one flips Steve's tray onto the floor, all his food.

Steve walks out to the Goth lot and Julie follows him. "Who cares about them," she says.

"Just back off," he says, and he won't say anything more the rest of the day.

The next day, though, he tells her, "I love school because I love working. But I hate school because of everyone in my classes. I hate everyone."

"You can't hate everyone," she tells him. "You don't hate me."

"No."

"So the others?"

"I do. Some people I wanna hurt."

BY THE FALL OF HIS JUNIOR YEAR, when Steve first attempts suicide, his life is already destroyed. And then it gets worse, steadily, month by month.

I can understand some parts of that life, including being an outcast. I finally left all my friends the fall of tenth grade. We were all in band, like Steve and his friend Adam, and we went on a field trip down to an amusement park in Southern California. I hated Ian VanTuyl by that point, had fantasies of killing him, shooting him with one of my rifles. He deserved it, in my opinion, and I hated all my other friends about half as much for going along with him. They were brutal to me, every day, constant humiliation. So on this trip, I finally got off the bus they were on and got on the other bus. This one was for all the cheerleaders and baton twirlers, so I wasn't exactly welcome there, either, but I knew a couple of them, and they invited me over to help me get away from my friends.

So that was it. I wandered school friendless for the next two weeks. At lunch and snack break, when everyone huddled into their groups, I felt exposed and awkward, like I had a target on me that said loser. And I felt my life sliding away, a sense of doom that I was destined to repeat what my father had done, as if his suicide had a kind of magnetic force. I didn't imagine it happening soon. I imagined growing old enough to get married and have kids, and then watching my life fall apart as my father's had, with infidelity and divorce, guilt and depression that would make me finally pull the trigger, fulfilling my fate. Doom is the only word that fits, and that feeling would last, waiting always in the background, for twenty years.

But after wandering friendless for those two weeks, I started hanging out with a new friend I'd met on the wrestling team, Galen Palmer, and he turned my life around for the better. He introduced me to his friends in drama, and I tried out to be in the after-school drama workshop, an unusual program run by a teacher who had studied with the Polish Laboratory Theatre. Instead of pretending to feel emotion or planning out gestures, the focus was on improvisation, on working indirectly through associations, such as making your voice sound like dry grass if the part called for sadness.

I wanted into this group badly. I wanted friends, and I wanted to belong. So at the auditions, I told the truth about my father for the first time. For three years, I had told everyone that he had died of cancer. His suicide just felt too shameful, a personal shame, something dirty. But to this group, I told the story of the day we found out, and they let me in. What it meant for the shape of my life was that instead of continuing to spiral down into a double life, things began to improve for me, and this is what never happened for Steve in high school. His life spiraled into drugs, medications, suicide attempts, sexual shame, bitter fights with his mother, threats of violence. It's hard to know how exactly it all happened. Who handed him a KKK card? Who was the man he first had sex with, and was it consensual? How was he able to plan his own suicide in advance and even sell his things? I've visited all the places he went during those times, I've talked with his friends and spent time with them, gone to their houses, but I just don't have the experience to really understand. I haven't been on those medications, for instance.

Prozac is the one antidepressant approved for use in teens, and it's famous for causing or heightening suicidal thoughts. Depakote may have been the drug that puffed Steve up and sent him to 300 pounds, though Lithium can have that effect, too. The main problem may have been that he was on cocktails, combinations of drugs, so who knows what all the effects were. Of all his symptoms over the years—psychotic episodes, hallucinations, paranoia, anxiety, violent rage, insomnia, checking behaviors, despair, etc.—which ones were his and which ones belonged to the medications? It's partly because of the drugs that Steve goes off the chart and I can no longer connect his life to my own. Terence wrote, "Nothing human is foreign to me," but a person on drugs becomes something different than human.

ON APRIL 8, 1997, Elk Grove High School denies a request by Steve's parents to have a case study evaluation. They give his parents a handbook on dealing with students with disabilities. By this point, Steve's parents see him as mentally disabled and are asking for help, but the school refuses to help. April 13, Steve overdoses on forty Ambien and slits his wrists. Hospitalized at Rush. In the fall of his senior year, November 4, 1997, he tells his mother he doesn't want to go to school anymore. They fight, he says he's not going, and then, at 11:00 p.m., he takes fifty Depakote, an entire bottle, and goes to sleep.

He's surprised to wake up in the morning. And he's able to get dressed, go to school, but his first teacher notices right away how drowsy he is, and he's taken to the nurse's office. "I want to die," he tells the nurse, according to the police report. "Life sucks." This time he's taken to Alexian Brothers Hospital. His mother arrives within an hour, but does this make a difference to him?

They keep him in for only three days, which his friends feel was too short a time, driven by insurance limitations. Two months later, he's back at Alexian again, January 10, 1998, for suicidal thoughts. Four days earlier, the cops stopped him, along with Pete Rachowsky, after a neighbor reported they were smoking marijuana. The next month, February 7 to 11, he's back again in Alexian. While he's there, on February 9, his father walks into the police station and tells them Pete Rachowsky is dealing acid, fake acid, marijuana, and something else he can't remember the name of. The information is from his son, Steve. Pete keeps his drugs hidden in his radio. Steve's father wants Pete and several other high-school dropout drug dealers kept away from his son.

Steve gets out of Alexian on February 11 and goes back the next day, February 12, for suicidal thoughts and violent mood swings. He's constantly up and down on all the meds, all over the place, a mess, and maybe he's scared, also, about what will happen with Pete. He takes 120 Depakote, enough that he really should be dead, but even that doesn't work.

Steve's father talks with the police again on March 2. He has more information now. Pete sells in Lions Park, near the high school, and keeps his drugs in the battery compartment of his Walkman. The police bust Pete for marijuana possession.

The next week, on March 10, after dinner, Steve fights with his mother about Pete. She doesn't want him hanging out with Pete anymore. He storms out at seven o'clock wearing his trench coat and jeans, and she calls the police to file a missing juvenile report and lists Steve as mentally disabled. "He suffers from depression," she tells them. "He didn't take his last two doses of medication."

He walks to John Frazetto's house, but John isn't home. The police call and find out he was there at 7:30. They call another friend, Mike Terpstra, who last saw Steve at 10:00 p.m. at Grove Junior High with Pete Rachowsky. They took off, and he doesn't know where. Two days later, on the twelfth, Steve's father tells the police Steve has returned and they'll handle the situation with a physician.

Steve goes back to his part-time job at the public library, where a lot of his friends work. He's a page, restacking books. Adam and another friend, Jim, work on the computers. Joe Russo is a janitor. But the next week, on March 17, Pete Rachowsky comes in. He has a court date the next day for possession of drugs, and he knows now where the information came from.

Pete corners Steve in the library. It's eight o'clock. The library has mostly cleared out. Pete is tall, reddish-brown hair, on fire. "For less than an ounce, I could get people to take care of you," he says.

"Leave me alone," Steve says, according to a complaint he files with the police. He's scared of Pete, wants this all on record. Pete steps closer, backs him against a wall. "I could have your house burned down. Easy enough to throw a brick through your window."

In June, at the end of his senior year, Steve's parents don't include his baby picture and a congratulatory note from the family in his yearbook. Joe Russo's parents do this, and Adam's parents, etc., but Steve's parents stopped filling in his "School Days" scrapbook years ago. They're afraid of their son.

Steve slits his wrists for graduation. And he sells all his stuff first, just like before his first suicide attempt. Always planning these things ahead of time. Adam gets Steve's bass for almost nothing, his Led Zep tablature and amp.

Steve lives, though, again, and what he graduates to is the group home, Mary Hill Residence in Chicago, run by Thresholds. This will become the worst period of his life.

But he can't get in right away. He has to turn eighteen first, in August, so he spends the summer living at home, working at Dominick's, a restaurant, twenty hours a week. His job history: three Halloweens working as a monster in a haunted house, three summers as a ride attendant at Pirate's Cove, three months as a cashier at Toys R Us, two months at McDonald's, two days at 7-11. Six months as a bagger at Jewel. His sister, Susan, is living at home, too, working as a secretary, like their mother. Steve has trouble getting up in the morning, won't clean his room, fights with his mom about this and is hospitalized again August 2 through 5 at Alexian, then dumped back home again, like human garbage.

HOW MUCH OF STEVE'S STORY IS ABOUT CLASS? He'll joke later, "I know I put the ass in classy." He grew up in a nice enough suburban neighborhood, but class is not only about money. It's also about education. Steve's parents were relatively uneducated, as were the parents of his friends.

My mother moved us to a new neighborhood at the end of my fifth-grade year, and though our new house wasn't much more expensive, the class change was enormous, and I noticed this mostly in the kinds of friends I had and the level of education of their parents. In the previous neighborhood, in the flats closer to downtown, one of my friends was Leonard Smith. His father was a windsurfer who had basically abandoned Leonard and Leonard's mother, so Leonard had an angry violent streak and a lot of free time on his hands. Some of his deeds were funny in retrospect, such as when he tried to smoke parsley flakes in binder paper and it flared up and burnt his eyebrows, but he didn't have limits, and we spent our time wandering drainage ditches, tunnels, and industrial sections. In fifth grade, at age ten, we French kissed with two girls on a dusty couch in a carport, and if my mother hadn't decided to move, my junior high and high school experiences would have headed further in that direction. Many kids in the neighborhood stole, fought, did drugs, and had sex as early as age ten.

I remember feeling as a kid that my life wasn't really my own, that it could be shaped and sent out of control by others. Not long before my father killed himself, he asked me to come live with him up in Fairbanks, Alaska, for the next school year, and I said no. I felt tremendous guilt about this after his suicide, of course, and wondered for at least a decade whether he might not have killed himself if I'd said yes. But I was afraid of Fairbanks, because in my summers there, I could see the kids I knew falling quickly into drugs and sex and crime, and I was afraid of who I might become. I was only thirteen, in seventh grade, but that's old enough to understand the momentum of a life, old enough to understand that we can become something we didn't want.

I think about this for Steve because he refused drugs at first. He was cautious and scared and didn't want to get into trouble. But three of his friends in his neighborhood became drug dealers, and it seems that almost everyone else used drugs. They became Goths without thinking about what that meant, and their parents didn't think enough about it, either. Steve and his friends listened to Marilyn Manson, watched horror movies, smoked, stole, blew off their homework (a high percentage of his close friends finished with a GED, even after spending an extra year in high school), and hated mainstream society just because that seemed cool. Being depressed and suicidal was also considered cool, according to Julie. Their parents, for whatever reason, didn't intervene early enough in the process. So although Steve and his friends seemed to come from somewhat privileged backgrounds, white and suburban and attending an award-winning high school, they were actually lower class, along with most Americans. Then Steve fell even further into the company of the mentally ill, a group considered not even a part of society, an invisible class with no aspirations or promise at all, for whom the days become unnumbered.

THE MARY HILL HOME is a narrow three-story brownstone, like the side tower on a castle with no castle attached. The street is narrow, lined with cars that have been dented up and beaten. A car parked out front has replaced panels of a different color. There's an urban park across the street, chain-link fence and playground structures.

Before Steve moves in, he takes a tour and has a thorough evaluation:

"DESCRIPTION OF MEMBER: Steve is a 17 y.o. Caucasian male who appears his stated age. He is tall and overweight. During his tour, Steve was very quiet and did not ask many questions. His thought form appeared normal and his affect flat. He did not exhibit any bizarre or inappropriate behaviors during his tour.

"MEDICATIONS: Steve is currently taking Prozac 20 mg in the a.m., Zyprexa 10 mg at hs [hour of sleep] and Depakote 500 mg in the a.m. and 100 mg at hs. Past medications include Paxil, Cogentin, Risperdal, Lithium and Cylert.

"SYMPTOMS: Steve stated that when symptomatic he becomes anxious, depressed and unable to sleep. He reports losing interest in all leisure activities, has suicidal thoughts and feels worthless."

They wake Steve early here. They monitor his medications so he can't overdose. They make him keep everything clean. They make him work in the kitchen. He's washing dishes, and they're getting paid to make him do this. Then it's off to therapy. Group problem-solving therapy, Mondays and Wednesdays. Vocational training on Fridays. Then all the one-on-one sessions.

Rather than getting better, his symptoms get worse. He's oversedated, overweight, doesn't want to take his meds. He has special powers, though, he tells his psychiatrist. He can see his old girlfriend, Missy. And he can read minds. He's been able to do this all his life, but the power is stronger now, for some reason. He knows what they think of him here, how they underestimate him. In group sessions, you don't need to be a mind-reader, the other residents so slow you can actually see them think, see each twitch of a thought, the forming of each word on their lips.

When I visit the Mary Hill Home, on a spring afternoon, I see one overweight young white guy in a sweatshirt ambling up to the house. I cross the street and meet him as he reaches the door.

"How do you like it here?" I ask him.

"It's really stupid," he says. "They don't really help you. They just throw groups at you. I'm losing my hair because of it." And he leans forward to show me. His red hair is in fact very thinned out, and he's young, so maybe this is from the meds, but mostly he just sounds crazy and dumb, and I think this is what infuriated Steve most about the place. He felt he didn't belong here.

Steve crawls through the days, through the months, the longest time of his life. Through the fall, through winter, every day unbearable, every day the same. He escapes several times, makes his way home to Elk Grove Village, to his parents' home, begs them to take him back. Every time they drive him back to Mary Hill. Steve blames his mom, calls her a whore, a bitch, a slut.

Why won't his parents take him back? Is his mother a monster who fattened him with horror films in his childhood then threw him away when he became frightening himself? Or is this far too simple? What was his father's role?

Steve hates the Mary Hill Residence and is afraid of the neighborhood. When they encourage him to go out, nearly everyone he sees is African American. He rings at the front door, and there's always a delay before someone comes to let him in. If he's ever chased, if someone is trying to kill him, this won't be fast enough. His racism doesn't start here—he had a KKK card years before—but it does intensify. He'll talk in later years about how much he hated this neighborhood, how much he hates affirmative action, the idea of helping these people. Did any of this come from his parents?

He listens to Marilyn Manson constantly now. Julie introduced him. She said it made her want to destroy stuff. It made her feel "really cool."

But to Steve it just feels like comfort, like going home. *I'm just a boy, playing the suicide king. Your world was killing me. Nothing heals. Nothing grows. We used to love ourselves. We used to love one another. My prescription's low. The world is so ugly now. I want to disappear. Our skin is glass. Yesterday was a million years ago. I know it's the last day on earth.*

Manson speaks to every part of Steve's life, including the possibility of mass murder, asking the question, *What If Suicide Kills?*

Steve is only marking time. But then something beautiful happens. Columbine, April 20, 1999. Steve reads books on the occult, obsessively, but this is better. They can't hide the news from him. Columbine is everywhere, on every newsstand, on the TV. Eric Harris and Dylan Klebold just like Steve and his friends a year ago in high school, in trench coats, in the cafeteria, making the jocks pay. A brilliant idea, the propane tanks. If only they had exploded. Like watching himself. A triumph. Going out with dignity, not rotting here.

Eric and Dylan planned their killings and suicides in advance, like Steve. And there was no limit, really, to how many people they were willing to kill. They set a small firebomb in a field half a mile away that was supposed to go off at 11:14 a.m. to distract and divert police and fire crews. Then the two propane tanks were supposed to explode in the cafeteria a few minutes later, at 11:17. The tanks had enough explosive power to destroy the cafeteria, killing everyone inside, and could even have made the library above collapse into the cafeteria. Eric and Dylan waited outside in two different vantage points at their cars, armed to shoot students as they fled. If the bombs had gone off and the school had evacuated toward the parking lot, they could have killed hundreds.

The propane bombs didn't go off, though, and nothing went as planned. Eric and Dylan missed most of the students they shot at, and Dylan didn't shoot much at all. One teacher thought they were just horsing around and went to tell them to knock it off. Students were told to hide under their desks, and Eric mocked this, said "peekaboo" to Cassie Bernall before shooting her in the head. He bent down so close to her that the recoil from his shotgun broke his nose. He and Dylan were as putzy as shooters could possibly be, the entire event a comedy of ridiculous errors if it weren't a tragedy, and it continued on for seventeen minutes of killing and another half hour of roaming aimlessly before suicide only because the police were even more pitiful, hiding outside, afraid to go in, protecting themselves. The one teacher who died, hours later, bled out because he wasn't evacuated in time. It was the worst possible emergency response.

But in Steve's mind, Eric and Dylan were somehow heroes. They took control, and ten days after the Columbine shooting, Steve decides he'll take control, too. He goes off his meds, and he scores some pot. On Sunday, he smokes a lot of pot. But then he feels so paranoid. He's outside, in the neighborhood, and he's panicking. He runs back to Mary Hill, pounds on the door, and tells them he has to go to the hospital. They tell him to calm down, but he insists on being taken to the hospital. He needs to feel safe.

Steve needs structure. He's not right. He's broken. They've broken him from all the meds, and he's just smart enough to know. He weeps about it. His life is tragic. His friends thought he was brilliant, but he just worked hard on his homework. His IQ is 100, just normal. Just smart enough to know how screwed up he is.

He pulls it together over time, the rigid daily routine, the long march. They place him in a job at Things Remembered, October 27, 1999, but it becomes the Christmas season, everyone shopping. It's too stressful. The pressure, all the people, all these little things they want to buy. Gnomes and cottages and angels. Kitties and puppies. He needs to do things in threes to make sure they're done, checks his apron is tied, checks it again, but he can't do that here. He has to do each thing just once, and everyone he works with is a moron. He argues, and it's his fault, of course, then they fire him, just three days before Christmas. Merry Christmas to you too.

By February 1, 2000, though, Thresholds decides somehow that Steve has things together enough to transition out of the residence day program into an SRO, a single room occupancy. He has his own room in a crappy building, and they all share a bathroom.

This is an even worse neighborhood. "His first night in the SRO was rough," says Jessica Baty, the person who will come to know him best in later years, his girlfriend and confessor. "I remember him telling me about how he heard gunshots and someone was pounding on his door, thinking that Steven was the previous occupant. Steven said that he put furniture in front of the door." He doesn't sleep. He hides in a corner and fears for his life.

They place him in a job at Walgreens, but he's fired after a month, on April 17, 2000, for poor attendance. He's hired at Osco, a pharmacy, in June, but he's self-conscious, decides to go off his meds to lose weight. He starts having hallucinations of his ex-girlfriend again. At noon on June 13, he overdoses on twenty Effexor. A social worker wakes him at 1:30 p.m., drives him to work, but by 6:00 p.m., his break time, he feels so bad he goes to the hospital. They keep him on for another month at Osco, then fire him.

Steve is angry all the time, and paranoid. He isn't hearing voices anymore, but he has to check doors over and over, and touch things. The physical world is a torture of meaning. Threes speak to him, almost prophetically, tell him what to do.

In August, he goes on vacation with his family to Wisconsin. He gets angry, is impatient, impulsive, and he's too sedated. He and his mother meet with a psychiatrist at the end of August, and they talk about the meds. He's not actively psychotic anymore, so they adjust the meds a bit, though he's still on Prozac, Depakote, Seroquel, and Clozaril. He becomes a bit less sleepy.

Steve starts work at K-Mart in September. He thinks people are following him, that they're against him, ganging up. He gets in arguments with his coworkers, anxious and emotional. He's working a night job at UPS, too, but he quits that because it's too physically demanding. He's feeling sleepy during the daytime but getting used to it.

He wakes up one morning and he's wet the bed. This freaks him out, but he tries to hide it. It happens again, and again, six or seven times. He's a bed wetter now, on top of everything else. They reduce the Clozaril, and that helps. He chooses more Seroquel and less Clozaril, even though it will make him sleepier. He can't be a bed wetter. He'd rather be a zombie.

He visits his sister in October at the University of Illinois, and he's determined to enroll there next fall. In the meantime, he'll enroll at

Truman College and get a couple courses under his belt. Maybe it's seeing people his age who are happy. People his age who aren't drugged out all the time. But at this point something seems to click in Steve. He's going to get out of here and do something with his life. He's not as drowsy anymore, but he uses three alarm clocks just to make sure he wakes up each day.

Steve loses his K-Mart job in November when he breaks his hand. It's in a group session, on November 6, 2000, and Steve feels another resident has insulted him, so he bumps him in the smoking area when the guy tries to block the door. The guy hits Steve in the face, then Steve breaks his hand hitting the guy several times in the head.

This isn't Steve's first fight. He reports to his therapist that he was beaten up "a lot" in high school, that he was often the subject of jokes and insults. And he pulled a knife on Adam that one time after the "wiretap." But what is his history of violence exactly? When does it begin, and how, and with whom? And how did he feel about fighting? Did he like it? He never talks about it in later years, doesn't write anything. But it shows a certain level of commitment to hit someone hard enough to break your hand, and hitting someone in the head shows intention clearly enough. Was he willing already to kill?

Steve looks forward to Thanksgiving with his family, four days at home, but it goes terribly. His sister tells him she hates him. His mother sends him away early. Then, when he tries to just pick up his money and cigarettes from the therapist, he gets blamed for everything. He tells them to fuck off, he'll leave the program and doesn't need therapy.

A few days later, though, he's contrite. He wants back in, sets up a therapy appointment. And he follows through with his plans for school, enrolls at Truman, a two-year community college, for several classes in January.

Steve charges ahead with school. He wants to succeed, wants to leave his psycho years behind. His therapists warn him that getting overinvolved in school and ignoring his mental health issues will lead to a "hard crash" that will undo everything he's accomplished. But Steve wants out of the system, finds ways to end this period of his life. He weans himself off his meds at the end of January 2001, and he hides this fact for five months in order to still collect his money. They believe he's still taking the pills. He reports nonexistent side-effects, begins living a double life. They think they still have him, but he's on his way out. He gets them annoyed enough they won't even want him. He humiliates a woman on the staff by playing music with sexually explicit lyrics. He quits seeing his therapist, shaves his head. He tattoos FTW, "Fuck The World," on his own skin. He complains about noise and sleeping, so they have to move him around.

Steve moves out and gets his own apartment on June 21. He breaks the news of the five-month lie to his case manager the next day. With pleasure. On June 29 they meet again, and Steve says he did fine without the meds. His case manager points out that over the last five and a half months, Steve has "held one job for three and a half weeks, quit school without earning credit, tattooed himself, continued to have no friends, and quit therapy, the job club, and the college support program." But he also says something else: he suggests they expedite Steve's discharge, since he's not willing to work with them anymore. Steve wants out of Thresholds, and now they want him to go.

Steve becomes the Chicago Department of Public Health's problem. They do an extensive evaluation, which isn't easy to do. "Client is a poor reporter of his past/current situation," they write, and indeed he is. He lies and hides constantly. Of his suicide attempts by cutting and overdose, "client states he did these for attention, that he learned this from peers in residential placements." But they know he was making the attempts in high school, before Mary Hill. "Client has not taken psych meds for six months, says he learned to wean himself off, feels better, stable now." They don't trust this, either, and they generally just don't like his low motivation for seeking help. "Every time I have a therapist, it ends up bad," he says. He finds therapists annoying. "Same old questions . . . how are you feeling, etc."

They do get Steve to talk about his past and his family. He says his sister, Susan, "wants to repress men," admits his grandfather's alcoholism, and admits he had a difficult childhood, was the "butt of jokes" and "beat up a lot in school." Still, though, the Chicago Department of Public Health decides they just can't handle him, and they determine that his family can afford private services. But Steve fixes the problem. He applies to the Army on September 5, 2001.

Steve needs this. So he checks "no" on his application for suicide attempts. No, also, for "evaluated or treated for a mental condition," "used illegal drugs or abused prescription drugs," "depression or excessive worry," "received counseling of any type," "frequent trouble sleeping," and "anxiety or panic attacks." They give him a $4,000 cash bonus and sign him up for the Army College Fund.

Steve will have to wait two weeks to enlist, and he hates waiting, but then 9-11 happens, so this keeps him busy. Better than Columbine, in a way, everyone talking about it. The camera angle for the Pentagon plane is odd. It seems staged. And where is all the wreckage, all the debris? It's an 80-ton plane. What are they hiding?

He's officially enlisted September 20, shipped off to Fort Sill, Oklahoma, for basic. This will become the happiest time of his life so far.

Steve doesn't get along with his bunkmate, but he loves everything else about the Army. All this structure, all the order. You can imagine how great a relief it must be from his OCD. No more insomnia. No more struggle to get up. No more worry about what to do with the day. Every minute is planned for him. He runs and runs and runs.

Every one of them a maggot, every one of them the same. No more worry about what others will think. No one is thinking anything about him. No minds to read because their minds are beaten flat. He keeps his locker neat, checks everything three times, wins praise for this. Obsessive compulsive disorders are a good thing here.

They train him how to shoot, how to kill without feeling anything. No emotional or psychological response, that's what they're looking for, and he can do this. He tells Jessica and his best friend "Mark" about it, even years later. A point of pride. "He did say that the military does desensitize for killing," Mark says. "He did say that. We talked about it a couple different times. It probably came up in our conversations about Columbine and whatnot. But he just said that the military desensitized. He's like, 'I've been trained to kill someone and not have the psychological effect. Don't think of them as a person.' So it does tie in directly. He did tell me that."

In the Army, Steve's not supposed to question anything. If you think about right or wrong, if you worry about morality or ethics or who you are or who they are, this could slow your trigger finger. It could break the chain of command. It could get your buddies killed, and it's mutiny, treason, traitorous. Don't think. Just kill when you're ordered to kill. He loves this, can't wait to kill some "ragheads."

The land is flat here, endless in all directions, and the inside of his mind feels like this for the first time, open, stretching on and on, a kind of wind that's blown all the anxiety away.

THE MILITARY HAS TRAINED most of our mass murderers, including Charles Whitman, the Texas tower shooter who killed fourteen and wounded thirty-one in 1966, the year I was born. He invented the school shooting, really, though he also murdered his mother and wife first, not limiting himself to school.

The military trains all its troops to kill without feeling anything, and so we should fear every American who has served in the military. But they aren't the only ones we have to fear, unfortunately. Eric Harris and Dylan Klebold of Columbine were high school killers bred from a gun culture that comes at least partly from hunting.

My own earliest memories are of guns and hunting. This was Ketchikan, Alaska, 1970, timber wolves slung across the bow of my father's boat, trapped and shot. Antlers I found in the rain forest behind our house, moose and mountain goat and Dall's rams that my father felt were too small to keep. Running through that rain forest at four years old, I imagined I was being chased by bear or wolf, sometimes falling through the false second floor of branches and ferns and decay, disappearing completely, climbing back out in panic. Always holding a toy gun or even just a piece of wood shaped like a gun.

At six or seven, in Northern California, my father finally gave me a Sheridan Bluestreak pellet rifle, powerful enough to kill squirrels if I hit them behind the shoulder. The giving of the gun was a ritual, my father's pride and pleasure as he showed me how to pump the gun, how to pull back the bolt. He even read a poem from Sturm, Ruger & Co. about a father and son, used it to teach me safety: never point a gun at anyone, always assume a gun is loaded but never leave a gun loaded, always keep the barrel pointed down. This was very soon after he and my mother had divorced, and we had only the weekends now. Roaming his ninety-acre ranch near Lakeport, California, one of those weekends, I didn't realize the rifle was pumped and loaded, and it fired as I walked. Luckily the barrel was pointed at the ground. But my father turned around, the disappointment clear on his face, and my shame was nearly unbearable.

The next year, when I was eight, he gave me a 20-gauge shotgun for hunting dove and quail. It made the squirrels easy, too, though I had some bad moments, shot a squirrel high up in the trees once, only wounded, and it actually screamed as it leaped from branch to branch. I shot twice more, but the single-shot gun was slow and the squirrel kept getting farther away and just kept screaming, in terrible pain. For some reason, though, this didn't turn me away from guns but felt like part of the grim reality of growing up, inevitable, as if this type of experience were a given that couldn't be turned away from. As if we were put here to hunt and kill, and the only true form of a day was to head off with a gun and a dog, hike into the hills for ten or twelve hours, and return with meat and stories. That shotgun became an extension of my body, carried everywhere, the solid heft of it, cold metal, a sense of purpose and belonging. I gazed at it in the evenings, daydreamed of it during the week at school, looked forward to when I'd head out again.

When I was nine my father gave me a .30-.30 Winchester lever-action carbine, the rifle used in all the westerns, and he went down on one knee when he presented it to me, holding it in both hands, as if it were a ceremonial sword. "This is the rifle I learned on," he said. "This is what we pass down through the family. The rifle I hunted with when I was a boy, the rifle I shot my first buck with, the rifle you'll shoot your first buck with. It's a good gun, an honest gun, with only a peep sight, no scope. You won't be shooting long range, and you'll need to hit the buck behind the shoulder."

He moved back to Alaska then, and when I visited, we flew into a remote lake by float plane, camped on a glacier, and slept with our rifles loaded, a shell in the chamber, beside our sleeping bags. "If a bear comes," he told me, "the bullet from a .30-.30 will only bounce off his skull or bury in his chest and not do anything. You'll have to hit him in the eye or in the mouth if he roars." There was no moon. We were the only humans for a couple hundred miles, and I lay awake imagining the bear attacking my father in the middle of the night while I tried to sight in on an eye in the darkness. This felt like the nature of our relationship: I saw him only during vacations now, and he would give me tasks that felt impossible, including making up for lost time. We were supposed to cram half a year into a week.

I shot my first buck at eleven. A rainy weekend in September 1978, on the White Ranch, our 640-acre hunting spread in Northern California. A two-hour drive from civilization, it was the entire side of a mountain, with high ridges, enormous glades, pine groves and springs, ponds and switchbacks, an old burned area, and even a "bear wallow." Our entire male family history was stored in that place. As our Jeep pickups crawled along the fire roads, my father and uncle and grandfather would tell me the stories of past hunts. The creek where Gary Lampson stepped on a small sleeping black bear. The stand of trees where my uncle once shot a spike—a buck with only one point on each side of its antlers, too young, illegal—wounded it, and then couldn't find it. Places of triumph and shame, places where all who had come before were remembered. All of our family, all of our family's friends.

My father flew down from Alaska every fall for this hunt. He was in his late thirties then, a dentist like his father, in years of despair leading toward his suicide. Grim-mouthed, hair receding, thin and strong, impatient. Everything in his life had somehow gone wrong, and his depression was something I had no way of understanding at my age. But he hadn't always been like this. He'd hunted here since he was a boy, and he was known then for being light-hearted, a joker. Whenever he came back, he could see each year recorded in the place, wonder at who he had become.

At eleven, though, I could think only of who I would become. Shooting my first buck was an initiation. California law said I wasn't allowed to kill a buck until I was twelve, but the same family law that gave me a pellet gun at seven, a 20-gauge shotgun at eight, and a .30-.30 carbine at nine said I was ready now.

I imagined sneaking up through pine trees or brush to make my first kill, but the weekend was rainy, so we hunted directly from the pickup. It felt unfair, even at eleven. The deer would be standing under the trees in the rain, flushed out from the brush. They didn't like to get wet. I stood in the back of the pickup with my father, holding on for the ruts and bumps. And when I saw the buck, hidden mostly by a stand of half a dozen thin trunks, I immediately felt pounding at my temples. Buck fever. Heart going like a hammer, no breath. The moment of killing something large, another mammal, something that can feel individual, that moment is not like any other. You could call it many things—brutal, wrong, irresistible, natural, unnatural—but what it felt like to me was straight out of Faulkner, the rush of blood and belonging, of love for my father. This was the largest moment of my life so far, the moment of being tested.

I saw two points on one side of the buck's horns, making it legal to shoot. I levered a shell in the chamber and raised the rifle, but my father put his hand on my shoulder.

"You have time," he told me. "Rest an elbow."

So I knelt in the bed, rested my left elbow on the side of the pickup, much more stable, and looked through the peep sight, lined it up with the deer's neck. I couldn't shoot the deer behind the shoulder because its body was hidden by the trees. I had only the neck, long and slim. And the sight was wavering back and forth.

I exhaled and slowly squeezed. The rifle fired, and the neck and head whipped down. I didn't even notice the hard kick or the explosion. I could smell sulfur, and I was leaping over the side of the pickup and running toward the buck. My father let out a whoop that was only for killing bucks, and it was for me this time, and then my uncle did it, and my grandfather, and I was yelping myself as I ran over ferns and fallen wood and rock. I charged through the stand and then I saw it.

Its eyes were still open, large brown eyes. A hole in its neck, red blood against soft white and brown hide. I wanted to be excited still, wanted to feel proud, wanted to belong, but seeing the deer lying there dead before me in the ferns seemed only terribly sad. This was the other side of Faulkner, conscience against the pull of blood. My father was there the next moment, his arm around me, praising me, and so I had to hide what I felt, and I told the tale of how I had aimed for the neck, beginning the story, the first of what would become dozens of tellings. I slit the deer with my Buck knife, a gift from my father, slit the length of its stomach, but not deep, not puncturing innards. It seemed a monstrous task. I had both hands up to my elbows in the blood and entrails, not the overpowering foul bile of a deer that's been gut shot but foul nonetheless, ripping out the heart and liver that I would have to eat to finish the kill, though luckily they could be fried up with a few onions first, not eaten raw. I pulled out everything and scraped blood, cut off testicles, then my father helped me drag it to the truck. He was grinning, impossibly happy and proud, all his despair gone, all his impatience. This was his moment even more than mine.

Back at camp, we hung the buck upside down from a pole and I skinned it, punching down between meat and hide with a fist. My uncle fried up the heart and liver, and then I was sitting at a wooden bench under a tin roof with a slice of heart on my plate. Two holes in the slice, one big, one smaller, two chambers. It was tough and tasted awful, but I was able to get it down. The liver was not so easy. Mushy and strong. I forced several swallows but managed to feed most of it to the dog under the table.

The next day, in the lower glades—wide expanses of dry yellow grass on an open hillside, fringed by sugar pines—I saw another buck. It was in short brush off to the side, a three-pointer this time, bigger. I aimed for the neck again but hit it in the spine, in the middle of its back. It fell down instantly. Head still up, looking around at us, but it couldn't move the rest of its body. So my father told me to walk up from behind and finish it off execution-style, one shot to the head from five feet away.

I remember that scene clearly. The big buck and its beautiful antlers, its gray-brown hide, the late-afternoon light casting long shadows. After all the rain, the air was clear and cool, distances compressed, even in close, as if through a View-Master. As if I were looking at this deer through a magnifying glass. I remember staring at the back of his head, the gray hide between his antlers, the individual hairs, white-tipped.

"Be careful not to hit the horns," my father told me.

I walked up very close behind that deer, leaned forward with my rifle raised, the barrel only a few feet from the back of his head, and he was waiting for it, terrified but unable to escape. I could smell him.

He'd turn his head around far enough to see me with a big brown eye, then turn away again to look at my father. I sighted in and pulled the trigger.

After that, I began missing deer, closing my eyes when I shot. And I also made up imaginary deer. The next fall, when we split up to hike down through brush, I imagined a deer leaping out in front of me. The blood came to my ears, my breath gone, and it was the same as a real buck. I levered a shell in and fired, imagined the buck leaped at just that moment, arcing over the bullet, and I fired again.

My father came running, arrived breathless. "Did you get it?"

"It got away," I said.

"Did you wound it?"

"I don't think so. It was leaping. It leaped right over the bullet."

My father and uncle and I spent an hour searching everywhere for blood as I retold the story several times, how the light looked on its hide, a big three-pointer.

My father would finally catch on, though. We were on an outcropping of rocks over the big burn, an area consumed by fire years before, with only shorter growth now. A buck leaped out from a draw and bounded across the hillside opposite us.

My father was hunting with his .300 magnum, and he was an excellent shot, but this deer was far away and moving fast and erratically, dodging bushes and rocks. I was firing, too, but only pointing the gun in the general direction, closing my eyes, and pulling the trigger. I opened my eyes in time to see one of my bullets lift a puff of dirt about fifty feet from the buck, and my father saw this, too. He paused, looked over at me, then fired again.

This was the last time we hunted, and we never talked about what happened.

I turned thirteen that fall, after the hunt, and I saw very little of my father. At Christmas, he was having troubles I didn't understand, crying himself to sleep at night. He wrote a strange letter to me about regret and the worthlessness of making money. At the beginning of March is when he asked whether I would come live with him in Fairbanks, Alaska, for the next school year, eighth grade.

Not long after I said no, my father called my stepmother. He was alone in Fairbanks in his new house, with no furniture, the ides of March, cold, sitting at a folding card table in the kitchen at the end of a day. He had broken up this second marriage the same way he had the first, by cheating with other women. And now my stepmother was moving on. She'd found another man and was thinking of marrying him. My father had other problems I would learn about later, including the IRS going after him for tax dodges in South American countries, failed investments in gold and a hardware store, unbearable sinus headaches that painkillers couldn't reach, in addition to all the guilt and despair and loneliness, and he told my stepmother, "I love you but I'm not going to live without you." She was working in a dentist's office in California, where she had moved after their divorce, and couldn't hear well. She had to duck behind the door with the phone and ask him to repeat what he had said. So he had to say again, "I love you but I'm not going to live without you." Then he put his .44 magnum handgun to his head, a caliber bought, like the .300 magnum, for grizzlies, capable of bringing a bear down at close range, and he pulled the trigger. She heard the dripping sounds as pieces of his head came off the ceiling and landed on the card table.

I stopped hunting after my father's suicide, but I inherited all his guns. Everything except the pistol. My uncle wanted to get rid of that, sold it right away. But that still left me with my father's .300 magnum rifle, the .30-.30 rifle, his 12-gauge shotgun, the 20-gauge shotgun, the pellet gun, and various odds and ends I had picked up, such as a pellet pistol and a pistol crossbow.

In my eighth-grade year of shooting out streetlights and living a double life, I tried to be the boy my father had wanted me to be. I joined the wrestling team, which he had always wanted me to do, and I was unflinching with his rifle. I sighted in on neighbors at night from the hills, but I also sighted in on them from my own room, from my bedroom windows in the afternoon, watched the man across the street swirl a glass of scotch in his living room. I could see every detail of his face through the scope, even a few dark hairs in his nostrils. Shell in the chamber, finger near the trigger, trained for execution.

ON DECEMBER 1, 2001, as he completes basic training, Steve is notified he'll be stationed at Fort Bliss, Texas, in the Sixth Air Defense Artillery Brigade. Fine with him. It doesn't matter where. And then something happens.

It's unclear exactly what triggers it—maybe Steve loses his temper. Maybe the Army was just late in processing his full background check. But the medical examiner finds out that Steve has been hospitalized in the past for psychotic episodes and suicide attempts. Steve is flagged.

On February 1, they pull him in for a psych exam. He's worried. What do they know? Is this normal, to be tested like this? He tries to get the doctor to tell him what's up, but he won't say anything.

Three days later, February 4, 2002, they cart him off to William Beaumont Army Medical Center, throw him in the Army nuthouse as a precaution against any suicide attempt. They tell him he's possibly a danger to himself or others. He asks them what all this is about, and they don't tell him until the next day. They've discovered he lied on his application, concealed his mental health history, his suicide attempts and his psychotic episodes, including hearing voices and hallucinations. He's going to be kicked out.

He tells them they can't do this. He's a good soldier, he's fine now, but they tell him it's a fraudulent enlistment, because he did it for monetary gain, for the cash bonus and the Army College Fund. He worries that he's going to get a dishonorable discharge, but they give him an uncharacterized discharge, an entry-level status separation.

On February 13, 2002, they dump him in his hometown, Elk Grove Village. No notifications to anyone that he might be a danger to himself or others, just dump him, as the Army does.

Steve is crushed about being kicked out. He could have spent his life in the military. It was home, finally. Everything was right. But he does understand that a kind of minor miracle has happened. After all the years of mental health treatment, he was headed straight into the shitter, but the Army has turned his life around. He's been off the meds for a year now, he's in good shape, his head is clear, and finally he can make something of himself. He applies to NIU, gets in, enrolls in the fall.

August 2002. Strange Steve, that's what they call him in the dorm. He knows they call him this, and it's because of his roommate, Ahron Mack. Ahron tells everyone Steve's a psycho.

They're in a double suite with three other guys in Stevenson Towers on campus. Steve takes his food from Stevenson Dining Hall, goes up to the room, sits at his desk and eats alone. Watches the news on CNN, but all he can think about is goddamn Sallie Mae. He's not going to have the money in time to pay his tuition.

He's busting his ass, every single day. He knows if he doesn't make it now, it's straight back to the SRO in Chicago. This is his one chance. No meds. No more Suicide Steve. But everyone's against him. Even Sallie Mae.

Ahron comes back from dinner, so Steve fires up the Xbox, puts in the earphones, plays Halo. He likes the sniper rifle best. Zoom in 5×, or 10×, one shot, one kill, clear across the canyon. You can see the vapor trail from the bullet. He's one of the marines.

Ahron tries to get Steve off Xbox, tries to get him out, but he refuses. Steve doesn't drink, doesn't smoke, won't leave the room except to eat, Ahron tells the police later.

At midnight, Steve takes a shower. He wears long sleeves every day, even when it's muggy and hot. He doesn't want anyone to see his tattoos, the homemade sword on his forearm. He showers when no one will see, keeps the light turned off, likes the darkness.

Steve can't sleep. Ahron snores. Everything about him is loud. But Steve can't sleep because he's thinking about Sallie Mae and thinking about everything that's due in his classes. Not tomorrow, not even next week, but for the entire semester. He goes over everything in his head, every midterm, every final coming up, every paper. It all has weight, heft, a physical presence pressing in on him, his mind a flatland still but the horizon building up, coming closer.

He feels hollow, also. He remembers beautiful dark brown skin, wants to touch it, wants to feel her again. He remembers her, jacks off and then feels lost. It was impossible, just from the way everyone looked at them when they went out. And they were right. It was an abomination. Phillip Schroeder, one of his suitemates, will tell police later that Steve "was struggling to recover from a former relationship. Apparently he had been involved in an interracial relationship with an African-American woman. However, the racial differences between them had created too much stress and strain on both of them." Another part of Steve's racism, to be drawn to what he said he hated? Another denial from a man who wanted not to be gay? Who was this woman, and how long were they together?

Ahron's alarm goes off, and Ahron doesn't wake up. He has some sort of condition where he doesn't wake up from sleeping. You can yell at him or even shake him, and he won't wake up. But he still sets the alarm, a little gift for Steve.

So Steve hucks tennis balls at his head, hard, and this finally wakes him up. Ahron is upset, has the nerve to complain. Steve turns on CNN, loud.

Steve has class that day in Cole Hall, a big auditorium. Three sections of seats for several hundred, two aisles between. The seats go right up to the wall in the side sections, a kind of trap. The two aisles the only way out. The professor is up on a stage. Music 220—Intro to Music. Steve listens.

Back at the dorm, he runs into Phillip, the only one of his suitemates he can really talk to. Ahron isn't around. Steve speaks quietly, but he's hurrying, tripping over his words, telling Phillip about Ted Bundy, about Jeffrey Dahmer, about Hitler. Amazing, the things they did, how they got away with it. The planning, and can you imagine actually eating human flesh? Frying it up like a steak? "He would talk about them as if he idolized them," Phillip wrote in his statement to police. "He was intrigued as to how they committed their murders and he would tell their stories to others over and over again."

Phillip is good to talk to. He listens. But then he says he has homework to do, breaks off the conversation just as they're really getting into

Hitler, and then there's dinner, and Steve is eating alone again, watching CNN. The news, always something, always some killing somewhere, some disaster. And the control. The façade of two parties, masking the real power brokers. But Steve can see. He can read between the lines. He's going to switch his major from computer science to political science. While he watches, he reads *Hunting Humans,* a book that covers many of the most famous mass murderers, or one of his gun magazines. Then he's back to studying.

The next day, he's on the phone again with Sallie Mae, screaming at them. He needs his tuition money now. They tell him spring semester isn't until January, months away, and he'll have the funds before then, but he tries to make their tiny little brains understand he needs the money now. Anything could happen.

Later, he talks with Phillip again, getting back to their conversation about Hitler and the others. "I told him to stop because I had already heard him tell me their stories too many times and I was tired of hearing them," recalls Phillip. He doesn't want to talk about Hitler or Bundy or Dahmer anymore.

Steve must think Ahron has gotten to Phillip. "Strange Steve." So to hell with them all. He'll move out, get a single. This is unbearable, especially Ahron, but Phillip and Tom, too, and everyone else on the floor. He needs his own room. He'll tell them he won't take anything else.

It's a long fight with housing, but he does finally get his way, before the end of the school year. He moves out.

And the next fall, 2003, things are much better. He takes Intro to Sociology in Cole Hall with Professor Jim Thomas. Thomas is an old guy, tall, with wild white hair. He asks questions. He puts them all on the spot. He makes them think. He challenges his own authority. "How can you subvert the power of the professor?" he asks. "If you're not happy with this power relationship, what can you do to affect it?" He's into "crim," which is criminology, studies prisons.

Steve realizes prisons are a way into understanding America. The average stay is only a year, but the country believes they can lock people away, toss the key. Human garbage, just like how he was treated, but he's back, he's here, and so is nearly everyone who's been incarcerated.

And nearly everyone who's served in the military. Thomas offers a way of understanding institutions, the history behind them, how they take shape. He's a softy, an old lefty, wants people rehabilitated, doesn't ask questions about Steve's past.

Steve takes two classes with Jim, drops by his office, feels uncomfortable calling him JT as the others do, but Jim encourages him, as he does with all his students, breaking down the barriers, questioning power. A small cinderblock office, yellowish, crowded with two gray metal desks, gray chairs, servers for running WebBoard, Unix, and the department site, filing cabinets, no extra space at all, slatted windows, but it feels homey, welcoming, safe. Jim keeps strawberry Crush in a small fridge. He lets his grad students have the run of the place, and Steve wants in, but he worries about offending, always feels like he's intruding. "In the first year or so, he was always apologetic, extremely deferential, and seemed sheepish about taking up my time," recalls Thomas. "He *always* asked: 'Is this ok if I . . . ??' I'd respond with something like, 'Steve, it's as much *your* office as mine—just don't turn off the Unix servers.'"

Thomas becomes a positive role model for Steve. Steve writes later, for a questionnaire for Mark, that Thomas "was effective because he led by example and pushed those around him to excel, whatever they did, and lived by the philosophy 'to each to his own ability.' He wasn't a communist, to be sure, as the quote may imply, but he did make you feel as though you were on an equal level with him, which I feel is a powerful quality of a leader. For a leader to make their underlings feel as though they are in the proverbial trenches with them, that is a powerful and unique ability for any charismatic leader to have."

I MEET JIM THOMAS FOR THE FIRST TIME on April 9, 2008, at his house in DeKalb. It's an older section of town, a small two-story. I talk with his wife Barbara, who is an artist. She's friendly and smart and interesting, but I can tell she's also worried about my coming here, wants to protect her husband after all he's been through with the media. Media trucks were on the lawn that first evening, and Jim finally interviewed with someone from the Associated Press, then appeared on CNN, but without showing his face.

Jim has agreed to meet with me partly because I'm a professor and memoirist, writing about suicide, not a reporter. And my intention at this point is to write about Steve primarily as a suicide, not as a murderer. I'm hoping to write something more sympathetic than other media. I don't yet know, of course, about his juvenile record or really anything else of his earlier story. I believe the accounts that he was a sweet grad student who snapped.

Jim drives me to campus and we park in the lot right next to Cole Hall. I'm surprised by this. I wasn't expecting something so direct right away. Jim was Steve's friend as well as mentor.

"He was very methodical, very careful," Jim tells me. "He would have parked as close as possible."

This is the first time Jim has been to Cole Hall since the shootings almost two months ago. There's no snow now, and that circular drive in front has a small pond in the middle, with lovely bridges. We peer in the windows (the building has remained closed as a crime scene), and I can see bloodstains on the floor, though no broken windows now. Flowers have been set outside.

I didn't ask for this tour, but Jim walks me through the scene, including Steve's earlier preparations. He took the sim card out of his phone, the hard drive out of his computer. Jim speculates that he might have been paying for meals with cash. The shooting was on Thursday, in a class that met Tuesdays and Thursdays, and Jim believes Steve must have come to check on Tuesday. "He would have taken a risk in doing that," Jim says. "He could have been recognized. He still knew a lot of people here."

It's cold out, Jim's breath steaming as he talks. He's tall and doesn't wear a hat, used to the weather here, but he looks fragile anyway because of this event and its effect on his life. What I admire is his courage to examine it head-on, trying to find out the truth despite how that feels.

"Jokes," he tells me. "That's a lot of how we've gotten through." And he shares some of these jokes. "People say I was his mentor, so I trained him to do this, but I tell them I must not have done a very good job, because if I had, a lot more people would be dead."

Everyone who knew Steve has been accused by media for almost two months now of missing warning signs. So their jokes reflect that.

We walk around the building to the back doors.

"I think he came in these back doors," Jim tells me, "and checked both auditoriums. One has a sound booth, but the other has a screening room, and that has a door onto the stage."

We both peer into the windows. We can't go inside, because Chief Grady of the NIU police has locked everything down. He won't meet to talk with me. His secretary slipped and told me that he's let other people tour the hall, but since then she hasn't even returned my calls.

Jim has rehearsed Steve's last actions over and over, and he talks about them sometimes in first person. "It makes perfect sense to remove the sim card. I would do that, too. And I would lock the bag in the hotel not to throw off police—because they could just cut through a bag—but because I know I'll be out during the day and don't want someone from the hotel finding all the ammunition."

"Why did he come back here?" I ask.

"He was returning here to Cole Hall because this is where it all began, his struggle to make something of himself through academic achievement after the group home." Jim tells me Steve always felt he wasn't worthy, and what he did with his final act was to annihilate all that achievement, giving in to that dim view of himself, making it true.

"The media hasn't caught on yet to the significance of the first-person shooter games Steve played," Jim says. "He would have checked out the auditorium ahead of time to make sure he staged his 'game' correctly. He was very methodical. He wouldn't have left anything to chance."

We walk to the student union next, very close by, and I grab a sandwich at Subway. Jim says he doesn't ever eat lunch. Then we walk to his office, where Steve often sat and worked and helped other students.

Jim says I'll get to meet Josh and other friends of Steve's from the American Correctional Association student group on Friday, when we tour a community corrections center in Chicago. He tells me that he and Josh used to joke, even in front of Steve, that "Steve must be a mass murderer, because he's so nice."

"He was so deferential and polite, respectful," Jim continues. "He was deferential to a fault, really. Josh and I tried to get him to relax, and he did open up and come out of his shell. He could be funny, and we got him to have a few drinks now and then."

The media reported that a paper on self-mutilation in prisons was coauthored by Jim, Josh, and Steve, because it seemed like one of those warning signs, but Jim tells me it was actually started by another author, Margaret Leaf. She and Jim were really the authors of the paper, Josh did the research, and Steve did a bit of research but was mostly the editor. "He'd admonish us with 'who wrote this?' and it was fun. He was good at putting everything together, all of our messy writing."

Then Jim sighs, shakes his head. "I would try to praise him and his work," he says, "but he always felt his work wasn't good enough. I tried to get him to submit a paper for a prize, but he wouldn't submit it. 'I don't want to embarrass myself,' Steve said, but it was a great paper. It could have won the prize."

"Where do you think his insecurity came from?" I ask.

"That doesn't necessarily come up directly in conversation," Jim says. "You can talk with someone for years and still not know some things."

MEETING JIM THOMAS improves Steve's life considerably. The fall of 2003 is much better for him than previous semesters. But he still has trouble sleeping, starting in October. By February 18, 2004, he finally goes in to see a doctor. Careful not to say anything about depression or anxiety, but just constantly thinking of things at bedtime. The doctor recommends he see a psychiatrist, of course, but that's the last thing Steve wants.

In the summer, he takes a statistics course at Harper College, just on the side, to get ready for a statistics course he'll be taking at NIU the next spring. He gets through the summer mostly, though, by playing first-person shooters online and reading about mass murderers and serial killers.

In fall 2004 he meets Mark, who has a half-burned Bush/Cheney American flag on his door. Steve is excited. "I could never do that," he says. He has an anti-Bush sticker, but a half-burned flag?

Mark is someone he can talk to, finally, about all of it—the methodology of Columbine, going through weapons choices, the plan, each step, what they could have done differently. Mark a fast talker, smart as hell, quiet and calm but well-versed in all this stuff. Randy Weaver, the Turner Diaries, Waco, Oklahoma. The federal government. There's a new angle here. Before it was Bundy, Dahmer, Hitler, and conspiracy was on the side, but the two can be brought together.

Libertarians, that's what "Greg" says they are. Another new friend. Steve convinces Greg to switch his major to political science. They talk about the individual. Steve's favorite author is Nietzsche. The superman, above moral code. Only the weak let themselves be ruled by morality. They talk about Firearms Owner ID (FOID) cards. "It's back to the days of the Hitler regime," Steve says. "The government is trying to track us."

Greg grew up in a hunting family, beaten once for using the wrong caliber on a pheasant. Watched his uncle slaughter a pig with a dull axe and had to finish it with a sledgehammer. He has good insight into how Columbine could have been improved. He agrees with Steve, also, on zero tolerance or respect for the NIU administration, for Sallie Mae and everyone else who controls us.

Steve's academic focus is shifting away from political science, though, toward sociology and criminology, because of Jim Thomas. Steve helps found the NIU chapter of the American Correctional Association on campus and becomes its treasurer and later VP. He gets Mark to join, even though he's in political science. This is when he tells Thomas, "I'm focusing strictly on academics. I want to make something of myself after the group home."

ON A SUNNY, COLD FRIDAY MORNING in April 2008, I drive to Chicago and park in front of a large warehouse that has been converted to lofts. Josh Stone comes downstairs to let me in. He looks like a large farm boy, with a red goatee. He's the current president of the NIU chapter of the American Correctional Association. I feel awkward, but I shouldn't. He's friendly and easy.

Josh leads me upstairs to Jim Thomas's loft, which has a narrow hallway and then opens into a bar–living room area with floor-to-ceiling windows and a fantastic view of the Chicago skyline. I meet Amy, Kathryn, Ilana, and Diana, all members of ACA. They're friendly, but I also know I have to be careful. This group has developed a code of silence. They've been hounded by TV crews at all hours and by one *Chicago Tribune* reporter for over a month. They're not willing to talk to media. But Jim has told all of them, in a blast email, that I'm *NOT MEDIA*. I've clarified this by letting everyone know that I'm writing a story for *Esquire* and a book, and I've also said my intention is to write a more sympathetic piece about Steve, looking at his final act primarily as a suicide.

"What a beautiful view!" I say, and for the next five hours, I don't breathe a word about Steve.

We've met to tour the Salvation Army's Community Corrections Center, the largest halfway house in the country, helping former inmates transition back into society. Amy has toured thirteen prisons so far. She and Josh tell me about a tour to Angola, a maximum security prison that holds a rodeo twice a year. They strap a poker chip onto a bull's forehead and all the inmates try to grab the chip to get fifty dollars. The inmates also play a poker game in the middle of the ring while a bull is let loose, and whoever is the last to remain sitting wins. They have monkeys strapped to dogs, inmates who have never ridden doubling up on horses, etc., and the whole thing is also a crafts fair.

We walk a few blocks, meet the Salvation Army program director for lunch, and then take the full tour, marching up and down narrow stairways and hallways, peeking in residents' rooms with closets full of protein powders, hearing about programming and challenges. This was Steve's field, criminology and corrections, and these were his friends, so I try to just soak it all in. The place was formerly a YWCA, and it feels like that, similar to a large, simple youth hostel in a city, only with a few more rules. I'm surprised to learn that the average time inmates stay in prison in the United States is only a year. And it's the work of places like this to undo all the negative behaviors inmates have learned during their year in a broken system.

Steve was in a group home with similar rules, and several others in the ACA have connections, also. Josh's brother was in and out of juvenile detention, for instance. "Whenever he was out, he had the stigma of being from juvie," Josh says, and this created an awful momentum. This is what brings Josh and others to want to do such selfless work, helping people change the momentum of their lives.

We walk to a café afterward for drinks, and now, after five hours, the group begins to talk about Steve. I'm all ears, but I don't ask questions. They say they thought it was someone else when they heard the shooter was a sociology grad student. There were several others, in fact, who seemed more likely to snap. "It couldn't have been Steve," Amy said. But then the group talks about how Steve dressed up for Halloween as Billy the Puppet, the doll from the SAW movies, which were his favorite.

"Do you think the gun he had was real?" Jim asks.

"Could be," Josh says. The others don't know, but they remember him carrying a pistol that night. "I can't believe the media hasn't found the photos of that costume," Josh says.

Afterward, I drive Josh home an hour to DeKalb, then have dinner with him and his wife and her friend. Josh tells me funny stories, how he was afraid of Disney World for years because his dad almost drowned him twice and lost him there. On a water ride, his dad leaned back to make it more exciting but that banged Josh's head into a piece of metal and he had to be fished out of the water and given CPR. Then Josh was trying to stand up on some kind of boogie board or surfboard and fell and it whacked him in the head and he was knocked out again and had to be dragged ashore. Then his parents lost him and he was found by a showgirl from the Horseshoe Saloon, and a guy in a sheriff's outfit with a star went and found his parents.

He also tells me grad school made Steve really anxious because there wasn't enough structure. "Steve liked being told what to do when, like in the group home." When he was assigned a paper or other work, he'd do it immediately, far ahead of Josh, and then still worry about it. "He was all about control." Josh also says that when Steve moved away to the new grad program at the University of Illinois in Urbana-Champaign, he lost his support network, all his friends in DeKalb. He didn't make new friends easily in the new school.

After the shooting, Josh was going around trying to help everybody, trying to be there for friends, and he was staying up all night drinking. He'd drink a full bottle of hard liquor and then wake up feeling even worse. He stopped, finally, when he almost gave his two-and-a-half-year-old daughter the wrong medication. That scared him enough to stop.

So this is how my first two weeks go. I visit Jim's classes, both undergrad and grad. I attend a conference the department holds on ethnography and learn that what I'm doing here is really an ethnography, trying to blend into this community. And I go to a candlelight vigil for the one-year anniversary of the Virginia Tech shootings.

The sociology grad students all stick together, and they watch yet again as Steve is erased from memorials. Commemorative bracelets are handed out, and there are only five beads, for his victims, no sixth bead. "It's like we're not allowed to grieve because of what he did," his friend Alexandra Chapman says. In the first days, she tried to remove a Columbine shirt that was stapled over Steve's memorial cross on campus. "It was really hard to remove, with all the staples, and then suddenly there was a camera and bright light right in my face. The world met him that day, a different Steve than we knew, and they all hated him."

I feel sorry for Alexandra and the others. They're going through suicide bereavement while the rest of the world is trying to make sense of a mass murder, hounding them for answers. And the truth is, they don't know anything. I see why CNN, the *Chicago Tribune*, the *New York*

Times, the *Washington Post*, and many others have gotten nowhere. Steve was a very private person. He hid everything important.

My last night in DeKalb, I go bowling with all the grad students, and after a few drinks, one of them mentions that her cousin, Julie Creamer, dated Steve in high school. "She and Steve lost their virginity together. They were both on lithium and bonded through having the same diagnosis. He was a Goth then, wearing all black, and he loved Marilyn Manson. Julie tells stories like he was violent at times, beating at a wall or something when he didn't do well on a test. You should give her a call."

IN THE FALL OF 2004, the same fall he meets Mark, Steve also has a new girlfriend, "Kim." An art student he describes as "eccentric," but he likes her. It's been a long time since he's had anyone. So now he's doing better socially.

He's sick from all the anxiety, though. "I had extended conversations with him regarding him and Kim," Mark says. "When they were together, I provided him with quite a bit of advice. He always says how stupid he was for this or that. He had very low confidence with relationships. And at the beginning he was very to himself, right? So, it was hard to get him to open up, but once you became friends with him, he didn't hold his cards as close—and that's one thing he complained about with me, that I always held my cards close."

Steve gets physically sick from the anxiety. Abdominal pain, nausea, diarrhea. His acne gets worse, too. His body betraying him yet again. He goes to the doctor on April 18, 2005, and the doctor tries again to get him to see a psychiatrist, for follow-up on his bipolar disorder, but Steve knows not to go in that direction.

Senior year, he aces his statistics course with Charles Cappel, toughest course out there, ends up number 3 out of 90. Doesn't mention the stats course he took at Harper College. He's a piece of shit anyway. He knows this. They may be fooled, but he's not fooled. Good grades aren't going to change anything.

He tries to hide all his stomach problems from Kim, his loose stool, his bulimia. Goes swimming in the ocean in Florida at the end of the summer, and the problems get worse. So he sees a doctor and is really nervous. Someday they're going to catch up to him. They're going to find out about his history, they're going to put him on meds again. It's only a matter of time.

The doctor tells him the tests are fine and his abdominal conditions are likely from stress or anxiety. Tries to talk about this, but

Steve is out of there. It's his senior year. He's not going to blow it now.

He wants to apply for grad school at the University of Illinois down in Champaign, but Kim wants him to stick around. They're going to live happily ever after. So fine. It's not as good a program here, but he applies to NIU for grad school, gets Thomas and Cappel and others to write him recommendations. Easy enough. He's a teaching assistant for Cappel, one of only two undergrads invited to do this.

And this is what he loves, finally. This is where he's not a fake, when he's helping students in the sociology lab. He's good at it. Everything calms down, all the anxiety, all the stress, all the checking, the paranoia, all of it. He's sitting in his chair and his breathing is regular, his body feels okay, his head is clear. Carefully groomed, long-sleeved shirt, normal. No tattoos showing, no trench coat. No slurred speech from meds. They come to him stressed out, but he's able to show them how to work the problems, able to calm them. He doesn't feel like an instructor. He feels like a healer. He spends as much time as they need, encourages them, inspires several of them, even, to apply for grad school. He affects their lives in a positive way, and they love him for it. All these cute young women, smiling at him, grateful.

"He is extremely patient and calm when tutoring students who are stressed out about statistics and the high standards imposed on them," writes Cappel. "He has the highest ethical and academic standards, he thinks abstractly and analytically, and relates at an emotional and empathetic level with others."

Another professor, Kristen Myers, is struck not only by Steve's work ethic but also his sensitivity. She reprimands Steve one day in class for talking, and he comes to her office afterward very apologetic and actually cries. "He was such a sweet, sensitive man. There isn't much room for men like that." She says he was good-natured, tenacious, and very together. "Steve wanted to impress me with his skills as a student. It meant so much to him that I was struck by his rare sincerity. This is how most of us at NIU saw him."

Steve tutors at Jim's office, too. Still worried he might be overstepping, but the work calms him.

His relationship with Kim does not calm him. Screaming matches at the end of the semester that can be heard by the entire floor. He rents an apartment in January 2006, out of the dorms. He's still with Kim, but getting a little distance, and he keeps in touch with Mark through online shooter games at night and emails about politics.

Things are not going to work with Kim. They break up February 27, 2006, the same day Jim Thomas recommends Steve for the Deans' Award. Steve and Kim begin a long battle over a plane ticket her family paid for him, and this ends in her filing a police report, worried he might damage her property or her family's property. She knows he's bipolar and has a juvenile record.

Steve wants to forget about Kim, though, because he's met someone new, Jessica Baty. "Even before Steven and I started dating, I felt drawn to him. The first time I remember seeing him was at Northern Illinois University in an undergraduate criminology course. Steven was tall, smart, and he always wore long sleeves. He would make me so frustrated in class because every time that I wanted to say something, Steven would always say it first. During lectures, I remember sitting across the room from him and just wondering about him. I wondered why he was so smart and why he said everything first. I wondered why he always wore long sleeves, even in the summer. When I asked someone about it, they didn't know either.

"Our interactions were limited to ACA meetings, group emails, and classes. It wasn't until we were seniors that Steven and I were brought together. He was a tutor in one of my sociology classes. One random day after class, I was walking to my next class and there was Steven, walking toward me, deep in conversation with a classmate. He was so involved in his conversation that he didn't notice that he was nudging me into a garbage can. After I stumbled, he paused and apologized to me and then he kept walking. I, however, felt as though I had been hit by a truck. It took me a minute to regain my composure, but by the time I thought of something to say, he was gone. That brief encounter shook me to my core.

"Later on that evening, I created an email account and sent Steven an anonymous email, asking him what a girl had to do to get his attention.

Steven thought it was a joke and named off some girls that might play such a joke on him. After some playful banter, we just began chatting. He wanted to know who I was and even though I really wanted to tell him, I told him that I was too embarrassed now to reveal my identity.

"The next morning, Steven emailed me and told me that he had a girlfriend. Steven said that he didn't mean to be disingenuous, but he was so intrigued. Naturally, I was disheartened, but our conversations were so great and we had so much in common, that I emailed him back. We shared our interests, academic and beyond. It was too bad that he had a girlfriend because we seemed perfect for each other. I mean, there were few people who didn't find my interest in crime and criminals abnormal.

"I dropped minor hints as to my identity because he still wanted to know who he was talking to, but I was even more embarrassed now that I knew about his girlfriend. However, he mentioned that he was not happy in his relationship and wanted to get out of it and I told him that I could empathize with how he felt. There was an upcoming ACA potluck and I asked him if he would be attending. He tried to convince me to come, but I declined because I wasn't ready for him to know who I was. After the potluck, Steven emailed me and made sure that he told me that he went alone, hoping that I would be there.

"Not long after, Steven told me that he had ended his relationship and it was hard, but he felt better and knew it was for the best. Steven and I shared some more information about ourselves, what we wanted to do after graduation, how classes were going. Steven knew that I was in one of the classes he tutored and after mentioning something about a class we were both taking, Steven was able to figure out who I was. He said that he was happy to be able to put a face to the emails. I was worried that things would become awkward and strange in class.

"The next morning in class, I raised my hand for help and Steven came over to help me. I thought that I was going to die of embarrassment because he was all business. He tapped his pen on the table next to me and as we were talking, he lost control of the pen and flung it at me. Both red-faced, we laughed and I told him that he didn't have to throw things at me. Steven gave me his great smile and he apologized.

After class, Steven sent me an email and told me that my nails looked nice (I had mentioned in an email the day before that I was painting my nails) and he liked my sweater. I didn't think he could get any greater; he paid attention to the little things.

"We didn't have a first date until a few weeks after our emails began. Being so studious, Steven's big plans for spring break were to write all the papers that were due at the end of the semester. I could not believe that he was going to sit in his dorm room, alone, and write papers that weren't due for two months.

"Over spring break, we graduated to telephone calls. Talking with Steven was so natural and we never ran out of things to say. One time we were on the phone, watching something on television, and my mom asked me if I was talking to Steven. She said that she could tell who was on the other end of the phone because of the big smile on my face."

Their first date is to a local DeKalb bar for a drink. "It was raining and I offered to pick him up at his dorm. Steven insisted that he would meet me there, but I was more stubborn and insistent than he was. Later, he would tell me that he was embarrassed that he didn't have a car and he didn't want me to know he had ridden his bike. We had a few drinks and shared our love for 80s hair-band music. Steven wore the worst shirt ever and he told me that he liked how my pink socks matched my sweater. We talked about our plans after graduation and the countdown to graduation. Steven told me how pretty I was and he made me laugh. After a few drinks, we walked to a 24-hour diner. We laughed as we stumbled down the street to the restaurant. It was so easy to talk to him and there was no tension or pretending to be someone else. That is one of my favorite things about Steven, he was always real, good or bad."

Steve wraps his arms around her, and it's like the rest of the world doesn't matter anymore. Their own little island.

They graduate together in May 2006 and make plans to attend NIU for graduate school in the fall. And then the impossible happens—more impossible than being off meds for five years straight. More impossible than finding an amazing girlfriend.

Steve wins the Deans' Award. This is the highest honor given to any undergraduate in the college.

"I only got it because of everything Jim has done and said for me," he tells Jessica, but she can tell he's proud. This is the highest achievement of his life, after all the struggle and hard work. It's unbelievable, how a life can shift from one point to another, from slitting his wrists at the end of high school, graduating into Mary Hill Home, to this moment now, graduating summa cum laude, winning the Deans' Award, moving on to grad school with Jessica.

I MEET JESSICA FOR THE FIRST TIME on Sunday, April 20, 2008, at the Olive Garden restaurant in Champaign. I wait in the lobby for a while, listening to the music of idealized Italy. I'm wondering whether Jessica is going to show. If I were her, I wouldn't. You can never trust someone who wants to tell a story. But then she walks in. It's like seeing a celebrity, after watching her on CNN. Her pale, open face, an oval of confusion and guilt and loss. Impossible to know what she was like before. She's a kind of ghost now, walking carefully, and she's brought a friend. "This is my friend Josh," she says. "He's here for moral support." It's a new Josh, not the one Steve knew, this one smaller, dark hair, quiet, mild as milk. I wonder whether he's the new boyfriend. I'm guessing I won't find out.

We're shown to a table, and I'm talking, trying to ease the tension, wondering how to put her at ease. So as we sit down, I talk about my father, about suicide bereavement, about how sorry I am she's having to go through all this. And all of this is true. I feel tremendously sorry for anyone heading down the early part of that long road. You can't see the end in sight. It's terrifying. And I see similarities between Steve and my father, especially the relentless feeling they both had, deep down, that they weren't good, that they were ultimately just pieces of shit.

"It's been an intense couple of weeks," I tell Jessica, "because I've had to reevaluate my father and look at him more generously in some ways. After twenty-eight years of suicide bereavement, you sort of feel like you're through with it, but it's amazing, even after years, there are new stages that come up as you learn new things. It's made me more sympathetic to that struggle he had, seeing it in someone else."

I offer Jessica the chance to write something herself for the *Esquire* article, her own voice presented directly. She could tell the story of how she first met Steve. "It's pretty awful," I tell her, "in the media and vigils and such, how he's been erased, and demonized by the media, and I think there's something valuable in trying to recover who he was and what everyone loved about him."

At this point, I don't yet know his story. I'm still thinking he was that sweet grad student who just inexplicably snapped, because I've spent two weeks with his friends and professors, all the people who loved him, all the people he hid his past from. It won't be until the next evening that I go bowling and am offered that first contact with one of his high school girlfriends, Julie Creamer.

So I feel sorry for Jessica at this dinner, and she gets teary-eyed several times. When I first mention the victims, for instance, and when I mention his cutting his arms, though I don't yet have any context for that. She's especially upset when I mention that Steve's memorial cross on campus was burned by someone. I thought she already knew this. She cries, and I feel awful for bringing it up.

But mostly, at this dinner, Jessica lies to me. She realizes I just don't know much yet, and so she lies about everything she possibly can. I ask, for instance, whether Steve was ever with a man, because one of the grad students mentioned that Steve had confessed having several encounters in high school, but Jessica tells me that's absolutely not true. She's so upset she's not eating her meal. It just sits there in front of her for a full three hours of conversation, and her friend Josh doesn't eat, either. Jessica has ordered a peach iced tea with slices of peaches in it, and she swirls these around with the straw. I believe her about everything, have no idea she's lying to me. I was feeling manipulative, bringing in my father and my own suicide bereavement, but Jessica is even better at this game than I am. Her tears are real, she tells a few real memories of Steve, she confirms just enough to make the lies and evasions invisible.

STEVE'S WINNING OF THE DEANS' AWARD is a triumph after all he's been through. His life is good now. He's in love with Jessica, graduating and looking forward to grad school, and he also wins a two-year paid internship in public administration with the village of Buffalo Grove, about sixty miles from DeKalb. "It was my first choice and I am ecstatic!" he writes to his friend Ashley Dorsey, who has been awarded a similar internship. "All the people that I've talked to from Buffalo have been wonderful!" He's just as enthusiastic about the graduate program, a master of public administration: "As Dr. Clarke said at the beginning of the fair on Friday, it's the first day of the rest of our lives and will be a fantastic two years+!"

Something doesn't work out at the Buffalo Grove job, though. The internship fits perfectly into Steve's job aspirations to become a city manager, and the annual salary of $27,000 will certainly help him through grad school, but in his first week, spent shadowing all the city's departments (fire, police, public works, etc.), his supervisor, Ghida Neukirch, writes that Steve is "extremely shy and appeared to have the deer in the headlights look." He's always nervous about new social environments, and he's not fitting in. He's drinking a lot of Red Bull. He's upset, also, that he's not doing more important policy work. And then, on June 2, 2006, he abruptly leaves, after less than two weeks. He quits the master in public administration program, also, and switches to a master in sociology.

These changes are abrupt, and looking back, they seem tremendously important. Public administration was something Steve was truly interested in, not just the influence of a good teacher. The fact that this road ended so quickly must have created a lot of anxiety about who he was and what he was going to do with his life.

But at the time, everything seems to work out, perhaps because sociology is easy for him. He has a good fall semester, 2006. He's tutoring students, working as a teaching assistant in statistics. He's good at this, and the students seek him out. One of them is Anne Marrin, who was given his internship at Buffalo Grove after he left. He's upset to learn that she's been assigned an important project there, something not offered to him. But otherwise everything is working out well. He's co-authoring the paper with Jim Thomas, Margaret Leaf, and Josh Stone on self-injury in women's prisons. Steve a cutter, but now he's writing about this from a distance, using his past for his future career. All is being transformed. Sociology is a safe haven.

Steve hangs out with Josh Stone in Jim Thomas's office. Josh and Jim try to get Steve to chill out. "Meet our friend Steve," they tell new folks, and then they give some variation on that mass-murderer line. "He must be a mass murderer, he's such a nice guy," or "he's too nice, he must be an axe murderer." Steve polite to a fault, apologetic always, but he starts to relax with Jim and Josh. They introduce him to a new world. Those stories of a poker chip on a bull's forehead, monkeys strapped to dogs. Josh's funny stories about Disney World, his confessions about his brother's time in juvie. Steve still doesn't reveal much about himself, but he feels at home with Jim and Josh. They get him to have a beer, get him to hang out and take some time off. He's happy, or as close to happy as he can be.

Then Steve's mother dies. A battle with ALS, Lou Gehrig's disease, a battle he didn't see much of. He hasn't been close to her in years. Thinks she hated him, was afraid of him. So he hated her, and now this. No time to make anything up.

He doesn't tell people about his mother's death, or show emotion. He doesn't take time off school and won't let Jessica go to the wake, but he calls her and tells her he wishes she was here.

Then more change. He's just started classes and now it looks like he isn't going to be able to stay at NIU for grad school. The university has lost faculty from its sociology department through attrition and stripped the advanced courses, especially in criminology. So Jim writes a recommendation letter for him again, and Steve and Jessica apply to the grad program in social work at the University of Illinois, three hours south in Champaign. A smart move academically, a necessary move, but why does he have to make this change now, when things are just starting to work out? He hates the idea of having to move to a new place, having to make new friends. He doesn't want to start over. He doesn't think he can.

Things are falling apart with Jessica, too. On again. Off again. Messy breakups for everyone to see. The most recent one, she came teary-eyed to Professor Myers's class, embarrassed him. It's his fault, but he doesn't want everyone to see. During one of the worst breakups, he tells her, "I'm going to buy a gun." She takes it as a suicide threat, but she doesn't know how close he really is. This is always the roughest time of year for him anyway, the holidays, because of his family, but especially this year.

He's eligible now to buy a gun. September marked five years out of the mental health system, so it won't show up anymore. He applies for his FOID card in December, gets it January 19, 2007.

He's anxious about his future, about what he's going to do for work. On Valentine's Day 2007, he lets Jim know he's passed his correctional officer testing. He bombed the LSAT in the fall, taking it too soon after his mother's death. The thing about grad school in social work, or an academic future in criminology, or a position as a correctional officer, is that these were never his fields. They're Jim's influence, the influence of a good teacher. Steve wanted to go into political science, so he's thinking again about public administration, still thinking he might try to run a city someday. Or law school if he retakes the LSAT and does better. But really, he has no idea.

He stops going to his classes. He doesn't need them anyway, since he'll be transferring to the new grad program at U of I and the coursework won't transfer over. He buys a Glock .45 caliber handgun on February 19, a powerful weapon. He buys a shotgun and another handgun the next month. Goes to the shooting range instead of school. He'll get Fs in his classes, but who cares.

Then Seung-Hui Cho kills thirty-two at Virginia Tech. April 16, 2007. Steve's excited. He's firing off emails. "Crazy," he tells Jessica, and sends her Cho's writings. He's all over this with Mark, studying everything. The writings, where Cho bought his guns, his mental health history, the photos, the planning, the timing, even his favorite song, "Shine" by Collective Soul, and "Mr. Brownstone" by Guns N' Roses, which Cho writes a short play about. Steve's been reading other books on mass murderers, serial killers, terrorists, and he and Mark have been discussing all of it, but Cho takes front and center.

"I think it was mostly a sociological interest," Mark says. "He was interested in what was going on in the mind of Cho, and why it was so successful, and how someone could do it, how they could pull it off." Steve tells Mark that Cho "obviously planned it out well," admires how he thought to chain the doors. All the careful planning, like Columbine. Just thrilling, all of it.

The truth is that Cho's actions could not have been planned. He shot and killed his first two victims in a coed residence hall on the Virginia Tech campus at about 7:15 a.m. Then he walked back to his dorm room next door. At this point, he must have been surprised that no one was after him yet. He spent the next two hours changing out of his clothes, putting together a media package for NBC news (mailed at 9:01 a.m.), and arming himself for another round. This was not a plan. It was an improvisation after there were no consequences from the first round. No one killed him, he wasn't trapped into suicide, and he was mentally ill, ready to continue killing, but this is not the same as "planning" or "success." The fact that Steve could find this scene exciting rather than pathetic and tragic shows that he was mentally ill. The fact that Mark still thinks in terms of "success" and still describes a killer's actions as "methodology" shows that he's mentally ill as well. That's one problem with the concept of "warning signs." What if all of a mass murderer's closest friends are a little bit crazy too? Steve had two email addresses that contained the word "Glock," but his friends thought that was normal.

Cho's next round starts with chaining the three main entrance doors to Norris Hall, then he peeks in a classroom twice, which is a myth that will be told later about Steve, transferred over from Cho's story. Then Cho just shoots people. Two semiautomatic handguns, firing 174 rounds in nine minutes. Everyone trapped at close range in classrooms, like shooting fish in a barrel. He was allowed to buy nineteen clips to fill with ammo ahead of time, 10 or 15 rounds each, buying from the same online supplier Steve will use, so reloading takes only an instant. Steve will choose one of the same guns, too, the Glock 19, and in both shootings, this will be the most deadly weapon (used also in the 2011 Giffords shooting and others).

How much have things really changed since Charles Whitman, the Texas tower sniper, bought an arsenal one day in 1966 and lugged it up the tower in a metal footlocker? While I was in DeKalb, the Illinois state legislature tried to pass a law that would have limited handgun purchases to one handgun per person per month, meaning a person could still buy a dozen pistols a year, just not all at once, but that effort was struck down, voted against by DeKalb's own representative.

Cho killed thirty-two people, wounded another twenty-three, then killed himself before police arrived. The deadliest rampage by a single gunman in U.S. history, and the whole thing was just stupid. There's nothing cool or interesting about Cho's "methodology." Buy a Glock 19, buy some extra clips, walk up to a classroom and shoot people. We still have nothing in place to stop anyone from doing this. It's an American right.

TWO MONTHS AFTER the Virginia Tech massacre, in June 2007, Steve and Jessica move to Champaign, rent an apartment together. Separate bedrooms. They're not a couple anymore. Relationships just don't work out for him. And renting an apartment with her is probably a bad idea. He feels awkward bringing other women over because Jessica gets jealous, but they save on rent, they can share books, and she's a good friend.

He's falling apart, though. He knows it, and Jessica knows it. He checks five times to make sure the car is locked, three times for the apartment door, checks the stove. He and Jessica drive somewhere, but he has to turn around, drive back to check again that the door is locked. He washes his hands twenty times a day, has to wash the remote for the TV if anyone else touches it, has to wash if Jessica's cat touches him, hates all the hair everywhere. He can't sleep, gets up to check again that he's paid all his bills, checks the alarm clock three times. He's anxious and worried about everything, paranoid. He doesn't feel safe. Misses his friends at NIU, misses Jim's office, misses the sociology lab. He has these mood swings, totally out of control, and he gets really irritable, picks fights with Jessica.

"You have to see someone," she tells him. "You need a mood stabilizer."

August 3, 2007, he checks himself in to McKinley Health Center on campus at the U of I. He's worried about confidentiality. He doesn't want this on his record. And he's not going to tell them much. He doesn't mention the mood swings. Or the suicide attempts. Or Prozac. Or the group home, or lying to his psychiatrists or hating therapy. He doesn't tell them much of anything. Just some anxiety, insomnia, checking behaviors. He says he's interested in medications, worried about weight gain. Doesn't mention his bulimia, though Jessica knows. She's noticed the cuts on his finger from stuffing it down his throat.

The next day, he realizes McKinley was a big mistake. It really will go on his FOID card, even with the way he's downplayed his history. He won't be able to buy guns anymore. He drives to Tony's Guns and Ammo, which is just Tony's house. Tony's black, which makes Steve uncomfortable, but he seems alright. Steve trades in his Glock .45, which is too big a caliber, too hard to handle if you want to get off a lot of shots and actually hit something. He also trades in his .22 caliber pistol, which is far too small (Cho used one, but it wasn't as effective as the other pistol), and his 20-gauge shotgun, which is wimpy compared to the 12-gauge shotgun he'll end up using. He buys a Sig-Sauer .380, one of the guns he'll later use in Cole Hall. It's powerful enough, but more importantly, it's reliable. It won't jam, he probably thinks. It's also fast. It's a police weapon.

He tells Jessica, "One day I might just disappear and nobody will ever find me." He's already told her, "If anything happens, don't tell anyone about me." If she weren't mentally ill herself, she might make some connections at this point. The spooky comments, the obsession over guns and killers, the time spent at the shooting range, the mental health problems. What does a mass murderer have to do to get noticed?

Steve debates returning to McKinley two days later, on August 6, but he really is falling apart, so he goes, tells a psychiatrist about all his "checking behaviors," how threes speak to him, guide him. He talks a lot about social anxiety. The move to a new school was a terrible idea.

"Steve shows elements of both social anxiety and obsessive/compulsive disorder," records the doctor who sees him. "My working diagnosis is Obsessive/Compulsive Disorder with the DSM-IV code 303.3. My plan is to start Prozac 10 mg each morning with breakfast." The doctor doesn't ask whether Steve owns a gun.

This is the first time Steve's been on Prozac in six and a half years.

But it's still not enough. Because now he's getting panic attacks. As he's sitting in one of his classes, his heart starts beating fast and hard. It's like a fist in there, balled up. He looks around, but no one seems to notice. He's short of breath, getting dizzy, disoriented. He's going to pass out, right here in front of everyone. He holds on to the desk, though, gets through the moment. His heart is still pounding, his breath still fast, but he's able to get up, gets out of there. No one will know. He's had panic attacks since high school, not very often, but they scare the shit out of him.

So now there's this on top of all the stomach problems. He has diarrhea, feels bloated, can't seem to get his stomach under control, and over-the-counter meds don't do much. His mother always said he had a nervous stomach.

He's also fighting with his sister, Susan. Their relationship has always been rough. She resented all the attention he sucked in high school, and he resented how perfect she seemed. But they have one good talk on the phone. He tells her, "I think I might be gay." She's gay, and perhaps he's reaching out to her. But peace between them never lasts long. The first of three tense and aggressive emails to her is on September 3, 2007:

"Susan, Just because Jessica and I aren't dating doesn't mean I don't care about her as a friend. Decisions that I make often impact her since we are roommates, and she has expressed interest in going to Florida in November, (although I am going alone to visit my father). Sometimes, it is very frustrating talking to you because you sometimes seem blinded by your personal outlook on life, relationships, and even family. If you are going to judge me and threaten to hang up on me when we talk on the phone, then don't bother calling. I don't need the additional stress/abuse in my life. The only people who I've ever known who were like this was my mother, and yourself. She used to hang up on me as well at times, (when I called from Chicago), and I don't need you to pull the same bullshit. You seem to get angry at the most petty things. If you want to know the real reason that I don't often want to hang out with you, it is because I often feel that you judge me and others, (i.e. my interest in working at a prison rather than finishing school, my relationships at times, etc.), and then you get incredibly mad at me for a decision that I own, and one that doesn't affect your life in the least. While this may be your function at work, it shouldn't be that way with family, especially your own brother. I'm not trying to quarrel with you, but this is something that I had to say."

Steve returns to McKinley the next day, on September 4, says his mother's death was a traumatic experience, still is. The doctor notes it in his evaluation. Steve worries, also, about his father, who has diabetes, hypertension, and a recent stroke.

Steve is anxious all the time in this new place, feels judged, worries what people think of him. He's hiding all the time, still doing well in his schoolwork, so no one would suspect. He did this at NIU, too. He's good at hiding. The doctor asks him whether he's planning to kill himself or anyone else. He says no. They up his Prozac from 10 to 50 milligrams a day and add Xanax, 0.5 milligrams a couple times a day as needed for anxiety. He's on Ambien, also.

He goes to dinner with Susan on 9-11, their mother's birthday. Susan thinks he's manic, paranoid, because he won't use his credit card. Someone could steal the number. So they fight again.

Steve wants to have sex. Right now, and with a lot of different partners. Is it because he hates his life? Is it because he doesn't want to be gay? Is it because of the medications? Prozac can reduce sex drive, but in a few people, it can intensify sex drive into radical promiscuity. Whatever the reason, Steve checks out Craigslist, posts an ad in Casual Encounters. "Katie" responds. She has 44Ds and is ten years older, thirty-seven, with "cushin for the pushin." He blows it, though. Makes some stupid half-joke about asking whether she's a cop. That gets her all paranoid, and she's put off.

It doesn't matter. There are plenty of others on Craigslist.

Steve starts his new job September 14, 2007, working as a correctional officer at Rockville Correctional Facility in Indiana. He's dropped classes for this job and isn't tutoring, either, or working as a research assistant. He's made sacrifices, and the job isn't what he expected. He enjoys parts of the training. They teach him how to use a Remington 870 12-gauge shotgun, the same model he'll use in Cole Hall. He has to take a test detailing how to load and unload it. He's fast at loading it. But he wanted to help people in this job, and instead he's just moving the inmates around from place to place. He has to hide his education from most of his coworkers, too. Being in a master's program is a kind of stigma here.

On September 25, he's hanging out with two of his coworkers, Nancy Hu and Samantha Hack-Ritzo, and tells them it's the anniversary of his mother's death. He's just thinking about her. But because he sounds so oddly detached, Samantha tells him he should go to therapy, which he doesn't appreciate. He's taken himself off Prozac, because it's given him acne all over his face, neck, and back. Going off Prozac is worse than being on it, though. He's really anxious, and he's checking everything, all day and night, can hardly get out of the parking lot in the morning, has to check so many times that his car door is locked. And he's getting paranoid. His homemade sword tattoo on his forearm looks like a prison tattoo. So he has it covered by a skull with a dagger. The guy Jason who does it is good, has already covered Steve's old rose tattoo with a skull and flames.

Then something stupid happens, something maddening. He's driving to work, early in the morning, talking with Jessica on the phone, passing endless farmland, cornfields, barns, and he misses his turn, drives past. This job is ridiculously inflexible. If you're late even one minute on one day, you have to start over from scratch. Your couple of weeks in the training program are thrown out.

So he turns around and speeds back, 85 miles per hour in a 55 zone, and then sees the flashing lights, pulling him over. So that's it. Why shouldn't everything in his life fall apart?

He drives to Nick Eblen's house—Nick is a training officer and has been letting Steve crash here some nights to shorten the commute—and clears out all his stuff. He leaves a two-page apology note, over the top:

"Dear Nick and Susan, I wanted to thank you for your kindness, but I am, regretfully, unable to continue with IDOC or with my training due to poor judgment on my part. I sincerely apologize for any embarrassment or shame that I may have caused by my stupid actions. For this reason, I must resign/quit my position. What happened is as follows: This morning I accidentally drove past Putnamville due to driving in the wrong direction. Upon discovering my error, I drove at a high rate of speed in order to arrive at the training facility on time. I was pulled over for speeding by a Putnamville officer and was given a ticket for a very high amount. I was also held over for a short period of time and was already past the training deadline. It's clear that I lack good judgment and do not deserve to wear the CO uniform."

What Steve can't quite put into words, though, is how he's just doomed.

"I may have graduated at the top of my college class, but I now understand that book smarts don't translate into common sense. In college, and by past girlfriends, I was often told that I was too smart for my own good. I now understand what was meant by this comment. I have left the key you provided me as well as my training manual, cuffs, ID Badge, chits, and other equipment so it could be returned to you and the facility. Additionally, please do not pick up my paycheck next week, as I will have it mailed to my residence. I am very sorry that this happened, but I suppose it is a wakeup call for me. I take full responsibility for my actions, and am sorry to everyone whom I affected with my poor judgment. Again, thank you for your kindness. It is clear that I do not possess the necessary skills needed to be an effective CO, and I apologize for wasting your (and others) time. I hope that you will find it in your hearts to forgive me. I am ashamed that this happened, but only God knows why it happened. Sincerely, Steven Kazmierczak. P.S. Thank you for your kindness, and I am sorry that I did not work out."

Nick Eblen thinks it's odd how Steve "fell apart" from this seemingly minor event. After the shooting, he will tell police that Steve was a "neat freak," with his pants creased and personal hygiene products perfectly arranged. He will remember Steve as "military-minded," getting up at 4:30 a.m. to run, and "obsessed" with watching the news. He will tell police that "Kazmierczak had some very weird ways."

The reference to God is interesting, too. It's less than five months now until his shooting, and Steve is reverting back to who he was in junior high, his mother and her Catholicism a part of that.

Steve calls the prison and leaves a vague message, saying that he's in trouble, so the prison superintendant, Julie Stout, sends two people to look for him, asking them to drive the route he would have driven. When they don't find him, she contacts Illinois police and they go to his apartment in Champaign. They lecture him for wasting everyone's time, very pissed off. Steve is pissed off, too, and thinks they're ridiculous.

A COUPLE DAYS after Steve loses his prison job, he fights with his former NIU friends on WebBoard. It's an online discussion forum he still has access to. They're talking about sex offenders. There's a gay grad student at NIU who works with them and advocates for them, and this is a guy Steve respected. I meet with him in the student union at NIU, and he tells me about a discussion they had once. It was in one of the labs, a place they called the "zoo," and everyone else had cleared out. "He felt comfortable with me." Steve confessed his homosexual experiences. "I told him I would share some of my own skeletons in my closet, too, and we were going to have lunch or something."

But then Jessica is looking around online, because she works in rehabilitating juvenile sex offenders, and she finds this guy on the list. He's a former sex offender himself.

Steve exposes him as a hypocrite. Disgusting, a horrible, horrible person. Steve is vicious, relentless in his attacks. So vicious that Jim Thomas and Steve's friends are shocked by the whole exchange. This isn't the Steve they know. They can't make any sense of this.

They don't know Steve has gone off his Prozac. They didn't know he was on Prozac in the first place.

Steve has an appointment at McKinley on October 16. "Steve stated that he noticed a worsening of his anxiety and obsessive compulsive thoughts with the discontinuation of the Prozac." He's still hiding most things from his doctor, though, and lying. "Steve stated that he had decided to quit his job in Indiana. He stated that the commute was too far and the job was taking too much time from his studies."

Steve starts to spend a lot more time playing online shooter games with Mark. "Sometimes we wouldn't follow the rules in games, whether it be team killing people [killing your own team]. Or we would pretend we were gay. Steve would do that to see how people would treat you differently if you were gay. And Steve would set up different rules, like making it so you could kill only with grenades, things that were not the norm and would make people mad, just to see how far you could push people, and to see how threatening will they get."

They have voice communication set up online, so Mark can hear Jessica laughing in the background. It's fun. But Steve seems to be aware, also, that something is wrong. He decides to write a paper on the connection between video games and mental illness. On October 19, he sends Mark an email asking for help: "Hey, I was wondering . . . if you happen to stumble across any articles related to video games and mental health policy, please send them my way. I am specifically looking for articles/journal articles that relate violent video games to a predisposition to chemical disorders, (and actual legislation or law bridging these two concepts together . . . such as the Illinois Safe Games Act struck down as unconstitutional just a few years ago). I'm working on research in this area and I hope to get together a publishable paper within the next few months on this issue, (hey, who knows . . .). Anyway, I know you're a news junkie like I am, and would appreciate any forwards if you find anything."

"In Columbine," Mark says, "they were playing Doom, he was playing Counter Strike back in 2002–3, and Grand Theft Auto, which obviously is the most violent game, there's been studies done on video game violence, and maybe people with mental illness, they detach themselves from the emotional part? I don't know if that's true. There could be a combination. Maybe for some people it desensitizes. We would play Warhammer on PS3, Battlefield, Call of Duty 4, any of the team-based games. I didn't tell the cops that, because you guys are just going to twist it around. But he wrote a paper on mental illness and video games, so I'm wondering if he saw a connection and knew himself."

Steve's relationship with video games is complicated, also, by his feelings about money and self-worth: "He always felt that he didn't deserve things, material things," Mark says, "because of his financial situation before school. He didn't want to get into that situation again. In the group home, not having money. Spending money now on $300 game systems, maybe he felt he didn't deserve it, right? Maybe he was worried that he would fall back. He had a problem with holding onto video game systems. He got me into Xbox 260 back in 2006, we both bought systems and played online, and then he sold it, just one day, he got out of it for awhile, said he needed the money for car repairs, then bought a couple other systems, sold those, went through a couple different computers, laptops, desktops, then he got an Xbox again in 2007 and we got back online, because he enjoyed playing online with me, and then up until fall of 2007, then he said he had a problem with the Xbox (later admitted he just didn't feel he deserved it) and sold it, and he always had a fear that I'd get mad about that, so he wouldn't tell me." Steve sold all his things before his suicide attempts in high school.

"Then he got a PS3," Mark says, "which I didn't have, so we couldn't play online with each other, so he tried to convince me to get one. This time he said he saw a psychiatrist about his problem of not holding onto things. And he said she had me engrave my name onto the equipment so it's harder to get rid of. So he told me he was done, he was past that point, and he wasn't going to get rid of stuff, and he recognized that he had a fear of hanging onto objects, that he sold them. He said he was confident now and knew he was okay financially. On that Tuesday [February 12, 2008, two days before the shooting], I told him I'd get a PS3 soon."

Video games are not Steve's most powerful addiction, though. A few days after his October 19 email to Mark, he goes on a wild spree on Craigslist in the Erotic Services and Casual Encounters sections. He meets a male professor from the biochemistry department at another university. They give each other blowjobs in the car.

He meets others, including "Kelly," an undergrad at Eastern Illinois University in Charleston, Illinois. He describes himself, on October 22, as "very gentleman like and respectful in person, but have a wild side. I'm well educated and am confident in bed. I have a few tattoos, love giving oral, (in fact, I enjoy giving it more than any other act, even more than receiving . . . which I'm told is rare by guys), and don't discriminate when it comes to fuller figures, different ethnicities, etc. I am DD free, clean and am in great shape."

In a later email, he tells her, "We can meet at a coffee shop or something if that makes you more comfortable, but I can assure you that I'm not socially awkward or anything, (actually, I'm probably too social and talkative at times, but I know when to keep quiet, lol)." She says meeting in a public place first "isn't absolutely necessary as long as you don't plan to chop me up and store me in my freezer. So . . . don't do that. :)" He reassures her, "I'm not a serial killer/psycho or anything," and to seal the deal: "Just so you know, I am very oral, and love to give it . . . True story: I have a particularly strong tongue, as I used to play the Tenor Saxaphone when I was younger. I've never had any complaints :-)"

He drives to her apartment for sex on October 23, 2007. He has to share the bed with a dog, "a cranky old Yorkshire Terrier with a purple rhinestone collar and several missing teeth," as she describes it, so that's unfortunate. He's had an uneasy history with dogs. He wrote a poem at age ten about the first one that died, titled "MESHA": "Oh, yes! I remember the anxiety I felt when my dog perished into death. I remember when her beautiful lips used to lick me."

Kelly is cute, long blonde hair, round and busty and wholesome, a bit of a hippie, but he also teases her about being a redneck, coming from a small town. They have a similar dark sense of humor, love the macabre. They're both excited about SAW 4 coming out on Friday. He has a great time with her, fun sex, up all night. He tells her Jessica is just a roommate and ex-girlfriend who's jealous sometimes. He's been trying to get her to date other men, since her jealousy is a drag.

The next day he buys the SAW box set. "Jigsaw is on the cover in plastic," he tells Kelly in a goodnight email at 5:27 a.m., "so how cool is that???"

"Get something scary for Halloween!" Kelly writes. "Then maybe sometime I can have sex with you when you've got a scary mask on . . . also in a cemetery."

So Steve does exactly that. "I bought the Billy the Puppet Mask (i.e. the puppet from SAW) and it is creepy looking! Maybe I'll bring it up next time I'm out there to scare the hell out of you, haha. Ever want to have sex with the puppet from SAW? lol. I told you that I'm pretty sexually adventurous, and I wouldn't be opposed to the idea . . . Know any good cemeteries? ;-) I actually enjoy sex in random ass places, (although

I haven't done it that much), so let me know if you're ever interested, as I am up for anything and everything."

"The puppet mask sounds good," Kelly replies. "It creeps the hell out of me already. I'd hate looking out my peephole to see that, but creepy is good. :) I don't know any good cemeteries around here, but back home there is a really old scary one on the lake that I have been eyeing for a long time . . . Let me know if you find any around here! Also, any empty churches . . . I'm pretty much up for anything as well, so feel free to share any ideas you've got . . . It's nice to not have to worry that I will offend you or creep you out, because you are just as sick as I am!"

"I'm also glad that I don't have to sugar coat things and be PC around you," Steve writes—they love watching Maury, make jokes about sterilization of blacks, about watermelons, about hating Mexicans, etc.—"as I usually have to make an effort to mask my words and contain my dark sense of humor. Oh, and don't worry Kelly, I won't ruin the ending of SAW 4 for you or tell you that Jigsaw is really the father of . . . Okay, so I didn't see it yet, but it's still fun to speculate as to how the series will conclude, (if it will conclude). I honestly wouldn't mind [if] the creators kept sticking to the recipe of another Halloween, another SAW since the series is *that* good."

Steve and Kelly consider sex in a public bathroom, and then Steve writes about Jessica: "Anyway, I can't wait until my lease expires here, as I'm going to start looking for a new one bedroom for next year. My roommate is great and everything, but I just want my own place, as I'm not really used to living with a roommate, particularly one that I used to date."

Kelly invites Steve to her family Thanksgiving in her hometown, but he isn't interested and she backs away from the idea, saying she just didn't want him to be alone for the holiday.

SAW 4 OPENING NIGHT, Friday, October 26, 2007. Steve is excited. He's seeing it with Jessica and Susan. A chance to make up with Susan, perhaps, and Jessica. Just had one of his fights with Jessica. He wrote to Mark, on October 24: "Crap on a stick! Jessica is flipping out tonight after too many drinks + prescription medication, so I won't be on until 11:00 pm [to play first person shooters online]." Jessica knows when he goes out to have sex, knows what's going on with Kelly.

But Susan is the one who really hates him. Maybe things can be better. Maybe they can get along. Susan is talking with a friend on the phone, though. Steve asks if she can drive, and she starts telling her friend how he's a jerk, and then he gets angry.

So no Susan after all. He gives away her ticket outside the theater. He doesn't know why it hits him so hard, not getting along with her. Family has always made him want to die. But to hell with them, he's going to enjoy the movie.

When he and Jessica enter the theatre, they smell puke. Someone has projectile vomited in the previous showing. Should be good.

The movie begins with an autopsy of Jigsaw, gruesome, sawing into his head, removing his brain, sawing into his chest, slicing through fat, removing his stomach. They cut open his stomach and find a tape. "Did you think the games would end with my death?"

The "games" are a kind of therapy. In all the SAW movies, Jigsaw is a pseudopsychologist, a man who doesn't have long to live (dying of terminal cancer), who is going to help his victims appreciate the value of life. He tells a rare survivor, "Congratulations. You are still alive. Most people are so ungrateful to be alive. But not you. Not anymore."

"He helped me," the victim then tells investigators.

All of Jigsaw's killings are strictly regulated by time limits and "rules." In the Cole Hall shootings, too, timing and strict control of behavior will help provide order to an insane act. Steve will walk calmly down the aisle shooting his victims, some of whom will be too paralyzed by fear to flee, then he'll turn around and march back to the stage to kill himself, with no hesitation. Like the military, the world of SAW offers behavioral control without any reference, grounded on absurdity. Unmoored from society, parroting the rules.

Later that night, Steve writes Susan an email, parts of which are meant to instruct: "Susan, I just wanted to let you know that I'm actually quite relieved knowing that things will never change with you, as it is clear that you do not want a change; only negativity and drama. I will leave you to your own narrow perception of the world, and wish you the best of luck without holding any ill will towards you. With that being said, I really need to let you know that I'm often shocked and appalled by your disrespect towards me, and always am disgusted by the way you talk to me. It's funny, because I've received more respect from hardened gang-bangers when I was in the group home. You are without a doubt the most rude and disrespectful person I have ever known, and it is unfortunate that you don't even realize it. In fact, I'm shocked that we are even from the same family, because we couldn't be more different. I mean, when you talk trash about me to your friends on the phone, simply for politely asking if you could drive to the movies, I know that we are not family; because family wouldn't treat each other in that fashion. Talking to you is analogous to walking over a mine field, and I was always constantly on eggshells when around you, for fear that I would say something that would trigger some negative reaction from you. What's most disturbing to me is that you don't see these issues at all and are therefore not getting the help you need. Even if ignorance is bliss, something has to give, Susan. Now don't get me wrong. I am far from perfect, and have never claimed to be. Perhaps I'm the most flawed human being in the world but that is irrelevant. The bottom line is that you need to accept responsibility for your actions and attitude."

Hints of Jigsaw, trying to teach Susan, letting her know she needs to help herself, just as Jigsaw makes his victims help themselves, whether that means crawling through razor wire, stabbing out their own eyes, or jumping into a pit of syringes. "Save as I save," Jigsaw says. "Judge as I judge." The flesh of no consequence.

"This is not about me at all," Steve continues in his email to Susan, "but rather deals with issues that you have ignored for too long. I really feel as though you have a lot of pent up hatred towards me due to our childhood, which is something that you need to seek professional help for. I am being serious and direct when I say this to you, Susan. There is obviously something seriously wrong when you feel the need to scream and yell at me for the most minor of things. I know a great deal of attention by our parents was diverted from you to myself when I was going through some rough times, and I often think you have issues with hostility, jealousy and self-worth, even today. Please don't take any of this the wrong way, as I'm just telling it like it is.

"Honestly, I think you need to sit back and re-evaluate your life, attitude, and the way in which you treat people. You are a mean and cruel person, and even if you surround yourself with dozens of superficial (and somewhat token) friends, you will still be that same person, no matter how obfuscated you wish your character traits to be. This can change over time, and I hope for your sake that it does. With that being said, I don't wish to be around you or converse with you any more than is necessary to conduct the business of the family, (i.e. at funerals and such). I really don't want anything to do with you at all. I don't need this stress in my life, and I'm amazed that even though I grew up over the years, you are still stuck as a petty and thoughtless person, trying to compensate for your inadequacies by disrespecting and belittling others around you. I can no longer even fake wanting to try to make amends with you or to make an effort to 'hang-out' with you, because I truly do not see the point when you are such an awful person to be around. I hope that you will eventually learn to be at peace with yourself and with those around you, even if it takes a great deal of time. Please feel free to save this email and to show it off to your partner, friends, and family members to curry sympathy and a shoulder to cry on. Play them for the fools that they are for buying into your melodramatic bullshit, because I am done with you. Good luck to you in the future Susan and I hope that you find whatever it is you are looking for in life."

Steve always lies awake from midnight until 2:30 or 3:00 a.m., so he has hours to mull everything over, to replay this email and all his rage at his sister, bottled up in his awkward formality and self-righteousness, but tonight, to make things worse, he wakes up at 4:30 a.m. He checks that the door is locked. The stove, too, checks that it's off, checks the fridge.

Then he checks his email and finds that he has a long one from Kelly. She calls him "oh-so-old-and-wise-one" because he has written to her that "No one's life turns out exactly the way they want it to, and it's just part of the human condition to want more for oneself." He confesses to her: "With respect to being wise, I am far from it, and if anything, I have realized how much little I know over the last few years of college, (yes, that's probably a totally improper use of commas, but I'm tired lol). What is the perfect, most immaculate life attainable by someone?" The word immaculate must reach back somehow to his mother, to that Catholic upbringing. Interesting that it shows up now when he tries to talk about happiness, and that he goes immediately to family. "The ideal type (of family) is a farce in itself due to the (somewhat) superficial view that normal, fully functioning families exist. I know, I know . . . let the cynicism abound! :-) I mention family when I talk with others and say that they are doing fine, but the truth is I really don't have much of a family. My justification is that I don't want to ever let people know this about me so they don't think I'm strange. It's rare that I even see members of my family. I'm not sure why I'm telling you all of this, but it's 4:45 a.m., so . . . let me rant about how fantastic SAW 4 is! My sister didn't end up going tonight. For Karma's sake, I gave somebody in line the free ticket to save them circa $8.00, lol."

The same day Steve found Kelly on Craigslist, he also found "Heather." Her photos don't show her face. Only her body, in lingerie. He meets her on October 27, the day after SAW 4, at a bar in Champaign called Phoenix, along with her sister and friends. "I usually don't drink," he tells her, which is true. He's currently on Celexa, after the Prozac didn't work, and Xanax and Ambien. But he has two white Russians. He and Heather split off from the group to another bar, the B DUB, then go to a hotel, the Econo Lodge. It's right off the freeway, the "crack and ho" section of town. They have sex. In the morning he's a gentleman, buys coffee and cigarettes.

Steve confesses everything to Jessica. He calls her at work, tells her he's not gay, then she comes home to find him a puddle of tears on the carpet. He's sobbing that she was here all along, and why couldn't he see that? He tells her about the male professor, about sex with three or four women.

He sees Heather again on October 30. Drives to where she lives, in Mattoon, Illinois, and brings a dozen roses and a couple movies. *Snakes on a Plane* and *Mr. Brooks*, about a good man who's actually a killer, carefully planning everything. She's not feeling well, though, so they don't have sex.

Halloween 2007.

Steve stands in his bedroom dressed all in black, with white gloves. The mask presides over his room, set carefully on top of his bookshelves, centered. Whited face, black hair, red eyes, red lips, like Marilyn Manson, but this is Billy the Puppet, a stand-in for the sadistic killer-narrator from the SAW movies. An old face, protruding cheeks and nose and chin, sunken folds between. A masculinized witch with red target circles on his cheeks. A clown, almost.

On the shelf below the mask, a miniature Billy the Puppet, full-bodied, a small doll. Framed above Steve's bed, a poster featuring the first three SAW films, along with movie facts.

Steve takes the mask down from his bookcase carefully, holds it to his left side, face turned toward him, a piece of himself, his alter ego. He and Jessica aren't going anywhere tonight. She's busy with work, and there's no love after his night away with Heather. They don't even get any trick or treaters.

Everything has fallen apart this fall, everything. His job in Rockville. Jim Thomas and his NIU friends on WebBoard. Jessica. Susan. The panic attack. Prozac and side effects. Craigslist. This is the beginning of the end. The final sequence, which will become as carefully planned and timed as any of Jigsaw's tortures.

Steve dresses up, puts the mask on. He's Jigsaw now, not only Billy the Puppet. He gets Jessica to take photos of him, arms outstretched, coming to get you, or holding a mallet cocked back, ready to swing. He emails the photos to his friends. Look at me. None of them know enough of his history, though. They think he's just dressing up. One of his classmates, Poppy Ann Graham, thinks it's "creepy—like there were two sides to Steve," in the one where he's looking at the mask.

After the photo shoot, perhaps he sits on his bed in his room, alone. Wears the mask, takes it off, studies it again. Gets up to check that his door is locked. Puts the mask back on. Is it sexual for him? It is for Jigsaw, though never acknowledged, so maybe it is for Steve. Does he jack off wearing the mask? Does he think of Kelly, in a cemetery or an empty church? Or maybe just looking at the mask, old witch, Marilyn Manson, mannequeen? Manson's body smooth, androgynous, shaven, and plucked. Steve plucks his eyebrows regularly, shaves his pubic hair.

Two days later, November 2, Steve has Jigsaw tattooed over his entire right forearm. He's not covering up an old tattoo, as he was with the skull and dagger. This is something new that he wants. He pays $700 for it. Jigsaw riding a tricycle through a pool of blood, with bloody cuts across Steve's forearm as background. He's a cutter, slit his wrists for three of his eight suicide attempts, and he needs to help himself, needs to learn the value of his life. Has he really learned? Every time he looks down, Jigsaw will be there, reminding him. "See what I see. Feel what I feel." Learning through sadism, through physical pain, through torture. An individual above moral code, like Nietzsche's superman, or libertarians like Steve, like Purdy who gunned down schoolchildren in Stockton, California with an AK-47.

Steve goes back to Tony's Guns and Ammo with Jessica. Just checking things out. She buys some pepper spray.

Steve asks Heather if she wants to go to Florida with him for Thanksgiving, to visit his father. They've been emailing five or ten times a day and talk on the phone all the time, usually for several hours after 9:00 p.m. She says no, worries he's becoming overly attached, tells him she's getting back together with her ex-boyfriend, so that's the end of that. Heartbreak, it seems, and he takes it out on Kelly, breaks up with her on November 9 by email, even though everything is going fine. The email is titled "Hey, everything is cool, but we were getting too close":

"Hey Kelly, I really like you as a person, so don't take me not answering your calls or emails personally, as you are a wonderful person, but

I'm not looking for a repeat with respect to sex; mainly because I've been in a lot of terrible relationships over the years and they always begin with sex—even friendly sex—but it always leads to more than I can deal with. Yes, I know it's dysfunctional, but it's just the way it is. Relationships and myself never really work out that well, as casual always leads to something else, and since we got along so well, this just compounds the situation. Seriously, I had a great time with you, and I really enjoyed your deviant sense of humor (which is rare in women), as well as the great sex, :-). I'm not trying to be a dick, but I don't know any other way of telling you these things, as I don't want you to feel bad or used or anything, but at the same time, I respect you and women in general, and don't want to be a stereotypical guy, which is why I'm emailing you despite the advice of a friend saying not to. I see that you posted on CL [Craigslist] again, (don't worry, I will never sell you out or anything, but am good at picking up on writing styles and such), and all I want to say is for you to be careful, and I would recommend getting pepper spray, as there are a lot of fucked up people out there. At least meet up in public next time like at a Coffee shop so you can be sure that the guy is not some basket case who just escaped from state custody or something."

STEVE KEEPS HITTING CRAIGSLIST, looking for sex. Mark writes to him, "Mysteriously disappearing, also known as Craigslist gone bad," because Steve is going off the radar.

Steve leads, usually, with that line about his saxophone tongue but settles in one case just for long chatty emails about school, life, etc. He spends a lot of time online with "Lisa," an undergrad at U of I, from November 6 to 7, 2007. They begin with a misunderstanding. Her ad on Craigslist, using the email name "damaged goods," apparently mentions a threesome, because he responds, "I've always wanted to be in a threesome as well and would be willing to participate as long as you are DD free (as I am) and can provide the 3rd person, (I want to be the one giving you oral)."

"I was just voicing my frustrations and fantasies," she writes back. "What kind of decent girl hooks up with people from craigslist? . . . if I were you I would stay away from girls soliciting sex on the internet, they generally fall into the category of 'whores.' By which I really mean 'dirty whores.'"

They work things out, though, and Steve ends up revealing a lot about himself, perhaps because he's pretty sure he's never going to meet her in person (though he does try). "I only have 2 friends who are male [Joe Russo and Mark], while the rest of my friends/acquaintances are female since it seems easier for me to click with someone of the opposite gender." He complains about the limited dating options in his program and says women in his field tend to be preachy. He tells her about being in a "state group-home," his history at NIU, that he spent all his time studying, resented fraternities and sororities, etc. She reveals that she came to U of I to be with someone she loved, which didn't work out, tells him about all her plans and hopes now, majoring in biology but considering the Peace Corps or the FBI.

It's in these emails with Lisa that Steve most clearly reveals his confusion about his career, about what he'll do with his life, and also how he felt about grad school. He details the shift from computer science to political science to sociology to law school to public administration. None of it has worked out for him. "I worked for a city manager as an intern for a few weeks and disliked it, because I could not tolerate working in a system that was so rigid and inflexible." He tells her about the cuts in criminology in the sociology department at NIU and says he's happy to have gotten into the social work master's program at U of I. "The odd thing is that I would have gone to graduate school at UIUC from the beginning if not for a woman that I was dating (an eccentric art teacher [Kim]) at the time who wanted me to stay in the area so we could live happily ever after, or something like that. Obviously, it didn't work out, so I kicked myself over that one for a while, but at least I'm here now. Okay, so you want to know the truth about graduate school? At NIU for my first year of graduate school, I was a teaching assistant for statistics, and although I enjoyed my teaching assistant position, I absolutely did not enjoy the graduate program. This was mainly due to the lack of quality students."

These are the same graduate students, his friends, who refuse to say anything negative about him even after he becomes a mass murderer.

Steve tries to meet with Lisa for coffee, but she refuses. "It's a shame that we didn't meet under different circumstances," he writes, "but such is life, I suppose."

Steve switches back to Prozac from Celexa, though only 20 milligrams instead of 50. The Celexa made him tired. And he looks forward to his Thanksgiving vacation, a chance to get away. He's going with Jessica, since Heather has dumped him and he's dumped Kelly.

During this Thanksgiving vacation, Steve shows Jessica all his mental-health records before destroying them. He insists she read them. He wants her to know everything.

They're in Lakeland, Florida, to help his father, who has gone into diabetic shock after a car accident. Steve writes an email to his sister on November 24:

"Susan I just wanted to let you know that our father is alright and that his accident may have been a bit over exaggerated by the family. I was down there, saw the vehicle, and read various reports (police, medical, etc.), and feel as though this incident should not be used to force our father to make decisions that he does not wish to make. When I spoke with you the other day and you brought up the idea of civil commitment, I was shocked and disappointed that something like this would be brought up, to say the least. Despite his accident, he remains both physically active and mentally competent, and I wish that you would stop trying to force his hand in HIS life decisions. He is a grown man and is entirely capable of deciding what he wants to do in the near future. If you EVER try to have him committed when he is both deemed to be medically and mentally competent by professionals, then I will see to it that you lose that battle, and I am willing to take it to court (hearing) if it gets that far. This is not a threat, but simply a reminder that you cannot force people to do something just because you feel it's in their best interest. As long as our father can carry out a normally live and is mentally competent, let him enjoy his hard earned retirement. The death of our mother is clouding your judgment, regardless of what you may say to the contrary.

"On another note, I saw that you and our mom acted swiftly (along with Russel) in 2005 to ensure that you had total control of Dad's decisions when he is unable to, (as well as his financials, etc.). Our father informed me of this when we went to the bank and during subsequent conversations. I do not care about the money or property (which you seem to obsess over, and therefore felt the need to go behind my back to gain control of), but I find it reprehensible that you would conspire with others to ensure that I didn't have any say in the wishes of our father once he passes. Have you no shame?

"While out in Florida, I had several conversations with Dad and learned that Mom never truly forgave me for being a 'bad/delinquent' teenager and that she never trusted me . . . even after I spent 4 years in college earning near perfect grades. Susan, I have had an epiphany while in Florida and now realize why you have so much pent up hatred again me as well! Punishing people for mistakes they have made in their pasts is shallow and shows a lack of character. I hope that once you obtain control over our father's property/money, that you get yourself a good therapist to work out these issues. Seriously, I mean that from the depths of my heart. After all, we are bound by blood, regardless of our current relationship (or a seeming lack thereof).

"Additionally, I was disappointed that you didn't even offer to drive us (Jessica and I) to the airport or offer to watch our cats. Jessica and I spent nearly a week watching your (and Carrie's) animals and spent our own money (for food and gas) to ensure that they were cared for. This does not even include having to get on my hands and knees to clean up dog crap in the kitchen/dog cage, either. All this, and you never even offered us a dime in return, or even an offer to watch our animals. How ungrateful can you and Carrie be? Obviously, family loyalty means little to you, or perhaps my definition of loyalty was learned somewhere else. Sometimes, I cannot believe that we share the same blood.

"P.S. (In case you're wondering, I prefer to email you rather than speak with you on the phone, because I have found out over the last few years of speaking with you that you often yell/get angry with me over petty issues; thus, I chose to email you instead). Happy Holidays, Steven Kazmierczak"

On the bright side, Steve's friend Joe Russo arrives after a couple days and they go with Jessica to Universal Studios. It's good to see Joe. Steve doesn't get to see him much anymore. They take goofy pictures, riding a cougar in the Wild West, wearing pigtails. Steve is wearing a black T-shirt that day with a handgun over an American flag. In the photos, he tries on several red, white, and blue hats to go with the shirt, and he also goes down a children's slide which is the giant skull of a longhorn. Perhaps this is the inspiration for a new tattoo he gets, of a skull with radiation, though Jessica says it was random, picked out by the tattoo artist. He and Jessica and Joe also go to a shooting range. One of his dad's neighbors, a friend named Joseph Lesek, takes them to Saddle Creek Park Pistol Range in Lakeland and loans them his gun. Lesek will tell police later that Steve "did not act or say anything out of the ordinary," but the ordinary in this case was to fire a pistol a bunch of times for fun, and the targets were most likely the outline of the upper body of a person. Lakeland a holdout for the Klan, still under a court order in the late eighties to desegregate their schools.

Steve has written a paper this semester titled "(NO) Crazies with Guns!": "I have only five words for you: From my cold, dead hands. Those words spoken by Charlton Heston, and immortalized by the popular press, have come to symbolize the pro-gun lobby's arguably firm and unshakeable ideology with respect to their opposition to anti-gun (whether real of perceived) legislation. With that being said, what if those so-called cold, dead hands happen to not only contain a firearm, but also a half-filled bottle of anti-psychotic drugs?" Steve thinks it's outrageous he's able to buy a gun.

In December, Steve is excited about AK-47s, which are more plentiful now in the United States. He seems reluctant, though, to buy a firearm illegally. The AK-47 was Purdy's choice for the schoolchildren in Stockton, California, on January 17, 1989, the day Ted Bundy was going to be electrocuted. A media stunt, stealing Bundy's fire. Nearly four hundred children were on the playground when Purdy bent his knees, braced the gun against his hip, and started sweeping back and forth with 7.62-millimeter bullets from a seventy-five-round drum magazine. He killed six-year-olds, eight-year-olds. The bullets had enough velocity to blast clear through the walls of the main school building. "They're just very cool guns," Steve tells Jessica. He knows about Purdy, and they have some similarities, including a similar racism and libertarianism, fueled by anger at the federal government. They're both poor, both obsessive-compulsive, violent in the past, run-ins with police, mental health problems, interested in Hezbollah, in horror movies. The similarities go on and on, actually. Mass murderers study each other, learn tips and tricks, help push each other over the edge. Virginia Tech helped prepare Steve, and then there will be another event, an execution-style murder of five in Chicago, that will provide the final turning point for Steve's shooting at NIU.

Steve and Jessica buy RockBand as an early apartment Christmas gift. They stay up for five hours one night playing it. Good fun.

Christmas 2007. Steve and Jessica drive to Susan's house. Cold out, and Steve wants to see his father, who is visiting from Florida, but he's vowed he'll never see Susan again. So Jessica walks to the door alone.

They take his father to a restaurant and this goes fine. They talk about school and how they've liked moving to Champaign. Then Steve wants to talk about how Susan has been pressuring his dad to sell his house and move back to Illinois. He tells his dad it's okay to stay in Lakeland. He shouldn't be pressured. Steve wants him to be happy. Susan shouldn't be trying to control his life.

The discussion is a bit tense. They switch the subject to Vegas, maybe going there in August. Then they go to Steve and Jessica's apartment, exchange gifts. They give his dad the first season of *The Sopranos*, watch a couple episodes together. It seems like it all goes well, but afterward, they need to drop his father off at Susan's.

Steve doesn't go to the door, but he sends along his present for Susan. It's a box of coal. Jessica laughed when he first told her, but she doesn't think it's funny now. He actually has a box of coal for Susan, wrapped in Christmas paper. After the shootings, Susan will tell police she's surprised he didn't come to kill her.

Two days after Christmas, Steve goes to Tony's Guns and Ammo, buys a Hi-Point .380, which he'll take to Cole Hall, and a 12-gauge shotgun. It's possible this is when he decides to do the shootings, though I believe the decision comes later, on February 3. But by Christmas, he's estranged from his family, and he isolates himself from his friends. Joe Russo tries to contact him around New Year's and doesn't hear back until February 12, two days before the shooting. Mark can't reach him for a couple weeks but receives a response on January 10: "Long time no chat," Steve writes. "Lot's been going on. Suppose I owe you an explanation for my disappearance. I had some family issues to deal with over the last few weeks, but I have distanced myself from the drama recently. Family, as you know, is a complex thing, and I've never had any kind of healthy relationship with mine. So why bother resolving 20-year issues when I'm out on my own? Not worth it."

"I never understood the extent of the issues," Mark says now, "because I didn't want to pry into his life."

ON JANUARY 7, 2008, Steve pays $395 for a tattoo of a pentagram, upside down star, sign of the devil. Jessica will tell police later that it's not that, it's just "antiestablishment." And what does that really mean? Is wanting to topple a real government less dangerous than wanting to align with a fictive being?

On January 11, Steve's back in touch with Kelly by email. She took the breaking up well in November, said it was a good thing, even:

"It's basically like we are both standing in a road and there's . . . oh let's say . . . a Greyhound bus barreling towards us. You're the one who looks at the bus coming closer and says 'Hmm . . . I have been hit by a bus before, and it sucked. I should move.' Unfortunately, I am the one who ends up standing in the road alone, staring at the bus and saying 'Well, I have been hit by a bus before, and I don't want to go through that again. However, maybe this time it won't hurt so much . . . I'm not sure if I want to take the chance or not.' So . . . what I'm saying is that in this situation, you had to be the one to shove me out of the road! It's really better for both of us in the end . . .

"As for CL [Craigslist], I haven't met anyone since and don't plan to anymore . . . I'm giving up on all that and have decided to actually let my vagina grow shut, as mentioned in my original rant. :) Too many weirdos. I know you worry about me, as I do also worry about you too (especially when I don't hear from you in days)."

In his email on January 11, Steve apologizes to Kelly: "Please don't take any offense that I didn't email you, as I had some family issues that needed to be sorted out, which is why I haven't responded or been in touch. I've always been good at disappearing like that, and I apologize. Also, I got too attached to you initially for a supposed CE [Casual Encounter, a section on Craigslist], but hopefully you understand. What can I say? You were fantastic."

Kelly responds positively, as usual, and they keep exchanging emails.

"Thanks for not holding a grudge against me," he writes. "Really, I'm a nice guy but can be a little odd at times. Stay macabre."

Steve sends Kelly a link for a joke song on YouTube, titled "I wanna be like Osama," that has a few odd echoes for the coming fame of his own mass murders only three weeks away now: "I know people will abhor me, but my God they won't ignore me." He tells her about "a religious right nutcase campaign to protest military funerals; their intent being to tie military deaths in Iraq to acts of god due to the United States (and their military, by proxy) supporting (or at least not opposing) homosexuality." He's gay and was in the military, but Kelly doesn't know. She thinks she knows him, but she doesn't, and this is the case for everyone else in his life, too, except maybe Jessica, who is in such deep denial she might as well not know.

Kelly tells him about a tattoo she's thinking of getting, based on a raven tree design on the Bounty Hunter website ("The Universal Federation of Contempt" is Bounty Hunter's tagline). Kelly wants to put "a quote from Nietzsche under it . . . 'You must become whoever you are' or whatever the exact wording is, however I want it in German."

"I like your tattoo idea," Steve replies, and of course he would. A reference to the superman, above moral code. "As it seems as if you've thought about it for a while. Are there any good artists around Charleston [in Illinois] that you plan on going to? There are plenty of shops up here at UIUC, but I'm loyal to a particular artist, whom I've gone to for my last 3 pieces of work. I brought in my ideas and let him work his magic with his freehand, (His name is Jason and he works at Altered Egos). I love the fact that Bounty Hunter is somewhat inspiring to you. Have you ever purchased any T-shirts from them? I have 3 that I picked up a while back; one of which I would probably never wear on an airplane, (the terrorist-ak-47 one)." This is the shirt he'll wear to Cole Hall. A black T-shirt with white letters that say "Terrorist," with a red graphic of an AK-47 underneath. In the same email he criticizes "the apologist theories which tend to follow the extremely liberal line of thinking, 'Don't blame me, blame society.'"

Steve is all about the individual, about the freedom of the individual above morality and above government. He writes to Kelly that "Big

Brother is watching you" and sends her a link to an article about new "secure driver's license" rules. This concern is shared by civil rights advocates, but Steve's focus is different.

"We are losing more freedoms by the day in the name of security," Steve writes to Mark, "and it's truly appalling. I hate both democrats and republicans alike. No one speaks for me anymore. Really, the invention of mutually exclusive ideologies in this country—liberal vs. conservative—has been a smokescreen for the real power brokers to utilize while achieving their own ends. Yes, it may sound like conspiracy, but it's the truth, although I would never mention it to someone in public lest I be labeled a tinfoil old hat paranoid radical. The media, like FOX, CNN, MTV all help to perpetrate the illusion of democracy by plastering pictures of racial apologists and bible thumpers all over TV on a 24/7 basis."

"This is just part of the conversation," Mark says. "You can see that he is smart, intelligent, and has a good viewpoint . . . More recently he started reading conspiracy theories, because we always talked half-jokingly about conspiracy theories and whatnot, but he said that he had some books and he's more into it. 9-11 for instance, some conspiracies about that, like whether the Pentagon crash really happened, because the way they had the camera angle, they had a camera that showed it, and then the way there was no debris left over for a big 80-ton plane . . . He wasn't a conspiracy theorist, but he just had interest in it. So that's an example of his intelligence . . . I really respected him for his viewpoints. He wasn't like a crazy tinfoil person. There was good theory behind what he said."

On January 16, Steve makes a joke to Kelly about "bleeding heart social workers," even though this is, theoretically, what he's trying to become. He's more interested, though, in gore. "I actually saw Sweeney Todd last night, and I HIGHLY recommend it. I'm sure the asian people in front of me thought I was a sociopath, as the murder scenes with splurting everywhere were hilarious!!!" Steve on the couch with his mother, watching horror movies all those dark afternoons. What did he see as he shot real people and watched their blood splurt? Did he think of it as "splurting"? Did he have that word in his head? Did it seem real? Was it different than what he expected? "There's even a song about how Sweeney and his partner plan on disposing of the bodies." Did he ever consider asking Kelly to be his partner? Another of Steve's favorite T-shirts: "Friends help you move. Real friends help you move bodies."

Steve and Kelly keep hitting the same topics in their emails—sex, gore, mass murder, race. "I just want to know why they all walk down the wrong side of the stairs," Kelly writes on January 17, "and when I am coming up them and they have to move, they shoot me a look like I just lynched their grandmother. True story, at least 2× per week. :)"

"Maybe because you were getting 'all up in they grillz.' I kid, I kid, but I know what you mean and had to deal with that when I lived in Chicago. Hey, stairs are important to protect, and hey, you never know . . . perhaps your cousin's mother's aunt's great grandfather's son's wife's mom lynched the grandma, (messed up family tree . . .). Better carry a strap and regulate!"

On January 18 they talk about "Jap rock." Steve writes, "I'd rather chew glass than listen to Jap rock for five minutes." Then they're on to lip piercing.

On January 20, Steve writes, "Last night . . . I bored myself to sleep by watching politics and fantasizing about world peace and brotherly love on the eve of MLK day. lol. On a totally other issue, completely out of the blue, I was wondering if you would ever be interested in getting together for . . . a . . . well, sex. Yeah, this is blunt and to the point, but I'm not one to beat around the bush, (no pun intended). I thought we were a great match last time, and I'm not really interested in doing the whole Craigslist thing again. I find you incredibly attractive (and sexy); we're both comfortable with each other's bodies; and we both trust each other, (you know, that we're both reasonably sane)."

Kelly's first response is lackluster: "As for the whole getting together for sex thing, that's really up to you. If I have to pick between being your friend and having sex with you (even really great sex), I'd still rather be your friend. However, if you're comfortable with both, so am I."

"Well, I can handle the whole being friends and 'having fun' thing," Steve writes back, "and wouldn't have any problem with it if you don't. I thought the sex was really fantastic with you, so I'd definitely be up for getting together again, at your convenience ;-) . . . If you supply the Type O

Negative, I'll supply the . . . well, the fun stuff! ;-) . . . I'm off to read some social work theory about how the man is holding everyone down . . ."

They keep emailing, making arrangements for sex and hitting their other favorite topics: "No tattoo on the neck yet," Kelly writes. "I've also told my mom that I am getting one on the palm of my hand that says, 'pay up, bitch' with some dollar signs. Mostly, I just enjoy torment- ing her." They're also talking about St. Louis, where she'll be visiting soon: "Honestly, the place is terrifying in the evenings. Especially being white. And not having a gun."

Like many other racists, Steve and Kelly don't know they're racist, don't realize how often they threaten violence, and are distracted by sex. Steve offers his place when Jessica will be at work, "in order to avoid a strange/uncomfortable situation."

On January 21, Kelly sends him an email joking that "my job is driv- ing me to the brink of a mass murder." Steve has been playing Call of Duty 4 online, says that "practicing with virtual weapons translates into?" and doesn't finish the thought. He calls her his 'homey' and writes "BTW-Homey Hopper was a derogatory term used on the Maury show to describe a white hooker who liked to get down with some Jungle Fever a bit too often. Hey, you asked!"

Their emails cool off again, which makes it seem they may have had sex on January 22 or 23, though Kelly denies this to police. So maybe something else is going on with Steve that takes him off the radar for a couple days. On the twenty-fourth, Kelly sends him an email trying to reconnect: "I know that maybe I'm kind of an intense person to be friends with. It's just that I have a lot to say and so few people that I feel like sharing it with. Anyway, I apologize cause I know that makes you uncomfortable/freaked out, like we are getting too close. I don't mind doing things on your terms, so don't feel bad telling me if I am being a bit too much, you need a few days, please leave you alone for a while because I am a weirdo, etc. The key words being to tell me these things, don't just go disappearing forever. Like an actual friend, I do worry about you. So, I just wanted to go ahead and tell you that, be- cause I think you're pretty awesome and I do want to be your friend. So . . . I will talk to you whenever! =)"

Steve replies that he didn't mean to give that impression and he wasn't planning on disappearing, but he remains breezy and distant, saying "Keep in touch."

Kelly goes out drinking with her friend Mina and sends him an email at 2:25 a.m. "Cause you know . . . it's not just for the homos anymore. So, my friend Mina and I just returned from karaoke night at the bar (and possibly one too many cranberry and vodkas . . .) and we have decided to launch a campaign to take back the rainbow . . . because dammit, we like rainbows and we don't want people thinking we are gay because of it. So join us in our worthy crusade! :) Are you free on Sunday morning? I was thinking that if you are, that would be a good time for you to come over. I don't work until 3pm! I was going to go to church, but I mean, I could be persuaded into staying home for some sex instead. So . . . let me know. :)"

What's it like for Steve to read this email? He's told his gay sister that he thinks he's gay. He's been with men. It's possible that sex with women is only a cover, a desire to be different than what he is. But no one in his life ever knows all of him, so he's often caught in this kind of conversation. His politics are the same contradictory mix. His friends at NIU think he's to the left and that he wants to go into social work because he wants to help people, believes in rehabilitation, etc. They can imagine him in support of the Rainbow Coalition. But really he thinks they're all naive bleeding heart liberals, and his own faith rests only on the individual, above morality, above social code, ultra–right wing. One time after he's been reading his copy of Nietzsche's *The Anti-Christ*, he sets it down and Jessica picks it up. This upsets him—he's really angry, it's a violation—and he tells her the book is "very personal." Nearly every sentence of *The Anti-Christ* is an incitement to mass murder. Many of my fellow professors disagree with that, but I studied German and the history of German thought, and I have no sympathy for the church (I'm an atheist), so I should theoretically be a good reader for this book, but I still think it's the single ugliest book ever written. Steve loved it. No morality, just kill, kill, kill. Assert your will because you're bigger and better.

Steve's response to Kelly's email is short and doesn't reveal much: "Take back the Rainbow for freedom and democracy! Perhaps it can be a future campaign platform? Sunday morning will not work for me, as I'll be too busy sacrificing virgins to the almighty dark lord Satan on that day. Well that, and I'll be in Schaumburg."

Steve contacts the Navy recruiter in Champaign a few days later, on January 28, and says he'd like to enlist, not as an officer, even though his college education would make that possible now. He wants to be a grunt, told what to do, every day structured, no decisions. Is this a last attempt to grab a lifeline? Does he know where he's headed otherwise? He and the recruiter, Nole Scoville, discuss his previous discharge and Prozac in the past, and it seems that nothing will actually prohibit Steve from reenlisting. "The applicant revealed to me that he had been an entry level separation from the Army for failure to adjust," reads Scoville's report. "He had also revealed that he had taken Prozac in the past but had been off the medication for 8 years. The applicant also told me that he had a screw in his knee. By our instruction there were no blueprinting hits that would immediately disqualify him."

Steve is careful during the call, and afterward he's worried. He didn't tell the recruiter that he's currently on Prozac. If he goes into a psychiatric exam and says he's taking Prozac, that will disqualify him, won't it? And they might take a blood test.

Steve needs to return to the military. He talks about law school, about public administration, about corrections, about academia, but he's lost. A safe, controlled environment, daily structure, that's what he needs. He knows this about himself.

So he stops taking the Prozac. He has to do that. And just like when he went off it in the fall, everything gets worse. His obsessive compulsive disorder, his checking behaviors, his anxiety. He only has to get through maybe three weeks of it, and then he should be clean for a drug test. Does he realize, though, that his Army history is likely to repeat, that the Navy will likely find out he's lied about mental health in his application? Does this add to the stress, his sense of doom, his inevitable failure?

STEVE SITS ON THE COUCH CRUISING CRAIGSLIST. He keeps the screen facing away from Jessica, closes it if she gets too close. Sometimes she's talking, and he doesn't even realize she's been talking. She says he's acting strange, won't get off his case until finally he admits he's off his meds.

Then she wants to know why, of course, and he tells her, and she thinks the military is a stupid waste of his education and intelligence. But he knows he's not really that smart. He's not going to make it in academia or law school or public administration. He could work in prisons, or be some other kind of social worker, but right now, that just sounds like hell.

On January 31, 2008, two weeks before his shooting, Steve sends Kelly a link to the V-Tech Rampage game, asking, "Have you seen this? It's old, but was amazingly controversial for some reason." Her response is odd: "No, I hadn't seen that and I can't imagine why that would be so controversial. I lost the first round." By first round, I think she means she's played the trial version of the game. "I forgot to shoot that girl," she continues, "and I was just going after all the black people. Sort of practice for what I would actually do in such a situation. =) Just kidding . . . ! Sorry to hear that school is so insane for you. I'm sure you're learning lots of useful and awesome stuff. When things calm down, maybe you can come for a visit and some 'stress relief' . . . and we can shoot at black people together!"

Steve replies by sending Kelly a link to snopes.com of "Misspelled Martin Luther King Day Signs," reading "I HAVE A DRAEM" and "I HAVE A DERAM."

Steve sends the link to V-Tech Rampage to Mark, also: "Some history: I originally played this game when it was released, but it has since been edited due to an apparent RIAA legal threat, (music copyright violation). The original songs were significant and have been transferred into 8 bit NES-style [Nintendo] music. In case you're curious, the original songs were "Shine" by Collective Soul and "Mr. Brownstone" by Guns N' Roses; the former was Cho's favorite song while the latter was (as you know) a short play written by Cho in one of his undergraduate classes. The last song should still be there, which is actually pretty funny if you listen to the whole thing, (it's a home-made song called Ke-Ke-Ke). The phrase Ke-Ke-Ke means LOL and is popular amongst Asian users of Starcraft. The significance of Ke-Ke-Ke here is lost on me, but the lyrics are hilarious and the hook isn't half bad . . . I used to play Starcraft online and get my ass kicked by Asians."

Steve and Kelly have a conversation about mass murder for the next three days, mixed up with sex and race. Steve sends her a link on February 1 to a story about a woman who microwaved her baby, asking "Defrost or Timed Cook?" and Kelly responds, "You should know that nothing much offends me, that's just kinda sad. makes we want to hunt down people and off them. then again, a lot of things have that effect on me . . . im off mon thru thu this week, so maybe we will both have a free day. sometime anyway! i have something i want to try, haha (note evil laugh . . .)"

"hmmm, you have me intrigued," Steve replies. "What do you want to try? You know I'm open to everything and anything, (especially creative ideas), as long as you don't leave me visible marks with the whips and chains. Monday may work, if the weather doesn't totally suck and if it's around the afternoon . . . ;-)."

"Well now, if I told you, that would ruin the fun . . . monday i have class until 2ish, so maybe after that will work. i promise no visible marks. i don't even have chains! a whip, yes. if you have anything you want to try, im game as well. unless it involves me being peed and/or pooped on. i have one that can only be done at night, and maybe when theres no snow and its less cold, and it involves a cemetery. im a creep :-)"

"The whole peeing/pooping thing is a bit out there," Steve replies. "and I only do that on weekends anyway. Seriously though, I am up for anything, even if it involves pain and/or water-boarding CIA style. After 2ish may work, so let me know what your preference is. Do you mean you have a 'whip' like the leather thing you used to beat people with, or a 'whip' as in a blinged out car like in Pimp My Ride? I'm not sure I understand you youngsters and your ebonics, so I wanted some clarification. A strange thing happened like a month ago. I did the whole 420 thing before going to a concert and it was fantastic . . . I forgot how fun it was. This isn't to say that I'm going to be a pothead or whatever, (I haven't done it since then), but I forgot how fun it was, lol. Drugs are bad Pacman. I've never 420'd and had 'stress relief' though, which may be fun ;-). Not sure if you're into that though. Besides, I don't have any hookups in Champaign, as it's been years since I've been into that whole scene. Just thinking . . . Sure, I like surprises, as long as they don't end up with me lying face down in a ditch, bound and gagged in a drug induced haze. That happens wayyyyy too often for my liking."

"I have never incorporated cia style water boarding into something erotic," Kelly writes, "but that would be festive. im more of a masochist. and I mean whip as in leather thing to beat people into submission witg. the go go beetle isn't quite a pimp ride . . . as for the smoking, it's a fun time, but that will have 2 wait until i find out about the job situation, because im betting they test, it being a rehab and all . . . lame. i actually would enjoy waking up face down in a ditch, bound and gagged, in a drug induced haze. that never happens to me. :-(my life is so boring."

"Well, I've never really been with a 'dominant' woman, although I've always fantasized about it!" Steve admits. "That would be something that I would love to do, (I mean, have done to me). I'm totally up for being ordered around, slapped, beat etc. and would definitely be interested in that, if you were serious, of course! I have a very high tolerance for pain, which is probably one of the reasons I'm addicted to tattoos, lol. Being dominated really turns me on for some reason. Typically during sex in the past, I've almost always had to be the dominant one, and always wanted to be told what to do and where to do it ;-). Hmmm, sorry, but I'm really turned on right now . . . too bad it's 12:31am, and you're probably at work, lol. . . . Rehab sounds fascinating. Will you be dealing with hardcore crack-heads and/or nappy headed hoes?" A reference to Don Imus. Steve is also a huge fan of Sean Hannity.

Steve emails Mark the same link about the microwaved baby. "Ding," he writes. Mark writes back, "I wonder if she used reheat or regular settings."

"Ordinarily I'd say reheat," Steve replies. "But then again, you'd have to factor in weight and size, so regular settings might have been preferred." He includes a link to a drink called "Dead Baby Recipe." "Do you think she had a drink of this the night before?"

"And I put lol tasteless," Mark says. "But it's just an example of our humor. It was nothing harmful, as far as that goes."

On February 1, Steve writes to Mark about conspiracy theories. "I didn't tell the detectives about this," Mark says. "I didn't know how relevant it would be, but he sent me—one of his conspiracy theories he asked about was Timothy McVeigh and all that whole thing with Oklahoma, and he attached the PDF for the Turner diaries."

"I recommend it," Steve writes, "if only to gain a better understanding of McVeigh and what drives the CIM (the Christian Identity Movement)" and then he adds, "haha, Ruby Ridge does refer to the Randy Weaver controversy, which also inspired McVeigh's actions. I'm just happy because I have it straight about Ruby Ridge." And then he sends Mark a link about Terry Nichols: "I know Wikipedia sucks, but I wanted to point out the waste of money that the Feds and states spent while pursuing the death penalty."

"What the Turner diaries are," Mark explains to me, "it's about the government taking the guns from people, basically." Mark reads a description of the book: "The Turner Diaries, by Andrew McDonald: what will you do when they come to take your guns? It's about Earl Turner and his fellow patriots, who face this question and are forced underground when the US government bans the private possession of firearms and stages the mass gun raids to round up the suspected gun owners."

As idiotic as it sounds, this is the real basis for the pro-gun lobby in America: right-wing libertarian paranoia that the federal government wants to enslave all its citizens and needs to take their guns away first before enacting the evil plan. I would just laugh and shrug it off, but this is a major force in mainstream American politics. How can that be? Who are we?

"It was one of those things where he sent it to me and said it would be interesting," Mark says, "and this is our humor, here: I put 'this is our motivation for our plan on 4/19.' Back to, I believe 4/19 was Columbine, or 4/20. Something was on 4/19. And then I quoted from Wikipedia, 'his neighbors reported he was spraying fertilizer on his lawn of his Kansas home on the morning of the explosion.' I put down: 'How would someone take notice of such a mundane activity such as lawn care on a seemingly normal day? Lol, media manipulation.' Because why would neighbors notice that someone was fertilizing a lawn?"

Mark and Steve call each other NIGGA in their emails, and race keeps coming up as an issue: "Steve wrote 'Nichols has been married twice, first to Lana Padilla,' and then I put, 'oh, I smell a dirty bomb conspiracy.' That ties back to Jose Padilla. Steve goes: 'lol at Padilla's dirty bomb reference. See, right-wing extremists and dirty ragheads'—please keep in mind, too, that he wasn't racist or anything like that—'are one in the same.'"

"We were equal opportunity offenders," Mark says. "We offended everyone by just [being] ourselves. Whether it be Americans or Middle Easterns, or blacks or whatever. We just talked about the stereotypical, whether it be whites, the red-necked trailer park people, just how dumb they act, you know what I mean? Not to be offensive, right? Or, even with the blacks. There's the respectable black professionals, like Obama, the people that are respectable, then there's people that live in the hood that just want to live off government welfare checks and all that. So those are the people that we took ahold of and just said, these are different issues in society. Like the terrorists in the middle east. He had, not a fascination, but he was interested in Hamas. He was interested in Hamas because they were a group that gives back and helps out."

Steve was especially angry at affirmative action. "Another thing he didn't like," Mark explains, "is that a lot of the minorities that come there [NIU] took it as a joke, right? And not necessarily minorities, but there were a lot of minorities that got on there because of—I forgot what the chance program was called, I don't know if they have something similar down in Florida, but in Illinois they have it where, it, uh, underprivileged inner city students, there's a certain percentage that has to be accepted to the university, okay? Steve looked at it that he was in the same place at one point as these inner city students and he accomplished it and he greatly valued his education and he achieved what he wanted, versus the other students who come and they make a joke out of it. They don't go to classes, they just hang out all day, and he didn't like that. And I didn't like that either. You know what I mean? But then if you look at that, then why didn't he go to a black center and shoot people, right?"

IN HIS EMAILS WITH KELLY on February 1, Steve begins to worry about privacy. According to Mark, this was always a concern for Steve: "Steve was kind of paranoid about things, I don't know why, but he would delete all the emails, always. But I never erased any."

"Well, I've always wondered if you show these emails to anyone," Steve writes to Kelly, "because that would be weird, but I don't really care, lol. Oh, I meant to mention . . . when I said I'm up for anything, I mean anything, even a 3 way (male or female) on the back of a train with hobos watching and fighting with home-made shanks over canned soup. It can be an erotic version of Bum-Fights or something. It's great that you want to be a CADC (not sure of the acronym at the moment), because it's not a bad profession. Druggies are fun and will provide you with many, many crazy stories to tell. Like that time where I snorted coke off a hooker's belly while tripping on LSD. j/k, but I'm sure you'd be a great counselor; particularly since you need a totally fucked up sense of humor for a job like that. I'm amazed at times how many of my fellow students, (whom want to be social workers), are so offended by everything and anything that's not pure, (whatever that means). Some of the people in my program were/are very sheltered. I'm a nick-name type person, so I just usually refer to odd people as nick-names. There's this one lady who I call Rated-G who is a bible thumper and is offended by curse words, violence, sexual references, etc. She verbally opposed watching a movie for social work, because the characters use words like 'Damn.' Seriously. She always talks about how she only lets her kids (and herself) watch G-rated movies and such, and is annoyed by some of my very vocal separation of church and state comments. Jesus freaks piss me off, as do most fundamentalists. But people like rated-G put the FUN in fundamentalist, I guess. All the worlds a stage meant for the entertainment of people with a bizarre sense of morality and humor, I suppose. Oh, To catch a predator is on right now, hence the name Hanson. I really want that show to be done in Illinois somewhere!"

Steve's feelings about religion come from his hatred of his mother, but it's interesting to note that you can be ultra–right wing and antireligious. The religious right isn't the only right. In fact, the ultra right is about the primacy of the individual, and so in its purest forms, it can't embrace religion, which is essentially against the individual. If religion weren't corrupt, it would be a force to the left in politics.

"That would be weird if I showed your emails to people," Kelly writes back. "You don't show them to anyone, do you? I only have a couple of friends who even know of the situation, and that was really only a precaution. I wanted them to know where to send the cops if I came up missing, hacked into pieces and put into an acid bath, etc. An erotic version of Bum Fights sounds amazing. I enjoy that show a lot. Especially that one loud crackhead with the fucked up teeth. I forget his name, but one of my best friends used to be able to imitate him pretty accurately. It was awesome. Was it Bling-Bling? Or did he just use that phrase a lot? Monday will likely work, but maybe 3 or 4? (That will give me time to shove my heap of laundry under my dresser, kick out all the homeless people that sleep in the corners, and hopefully plunge that dead fetus that has been clogging the toilet all week, etc. Should have just microwaved it, eh?) It's weird to meet in the afternoon, but since that's what works for you, I can probably skip my after-class nap for a day . . . Jesus freaks piss me off as well. Mostly because they refuse to respect the opinions of others most of the time. If 'g-rated' spent half an hour with me when I'm not playing nice, she'd likely have to be chemically sedated and committed. I have a way with people, you know . . . We should just do our own version of 'To Catch A Predator'! I'll do the dirty chat to lure them in, I have a friend who looks 13 to be our decoy, and you can be Chris Hanson. Instead of arresting them, we can taser them and then beat the shit out of them, leaving them in a ditch somewhere. Or whatever. It would be fun!"

"Okay, now I really am going to bed lol," Steve replies. "Sleep is difficult at times, but such is life. No, I don't ever show any emails to anyone, nor do I let anyone know where I am going, lol. Yeah, it may sound reckless, but it's not something that's an everyday occurrence. I can usually read and feel out people from the way they write, and would never meet up with someone who I didn't initially trust. I tend to be a fairly private person in general . . . The afternoon shouldn't be too unusual! The evening isn't the only time for stress relief!"

Steve and Kelly continue their emails later in the morning of February 2: "Well, you're probably safe to trust me," Kelly writes. "You should know that I really only kill minorities and children. I just give a vague explanation of the situation, really. It would be awkward to have to explain it. :) . . . I really don't want to have to work tonight. Those tards better be on their best behavior. (And yes, I am aware that 'tard' is not the pc term these days . . .)."

"Well, give me a call later if you're bored at work," Steve writes. "I should answer, as long as I'm not in the middle of preparing the acid bath. The garbage disposal is just not cutting it anymore. Oh yeah, I was watching this movie on cable the other day called 'Drive Thru' where the villain was a disgruntled fast food mascot. It started off hilarious, with a bunch of wiggers going through a drive thru late at night and getting slaughtered, (one of them gets his face deep-fried), but then (unfortunately) started to take itself too seriously. I love, LOVE B-movies, but not ones that try to be serious after showing cool kill scenes. Also, you should check out the new Rambo, if only to see the gratuitous violence and hidden messages, (i.e. patriotism good, god good, violence good, pedophilia bad . . . seriously there messages strewn through Rambo and it is incredibly comical at times). It's a Lionsgate distributed film (the film distributors of SAW and many other great movies), and it was entertaining. Probably the most violent movie I've seen in years. If you're into shockingly violent movies (with a minor message at the end) see Cannibal Holocaust. Besides having the best movie title ever, it was made in 1979 and is still the most violent, graphic, and craziest movie I've ever seen in my life. Nothing tops it!"

Why is this the best movie title ever? Is it the combination of Nazi and horror, the chopping of bodies in fantasy and in real life brought together?

"Garbage disposals clog too easily on the big parts," Kelly replies. "You have mentioned the Cannibal Holocaust movie before. I want to see it, but I'm not sure where to find such a film. :) . . . How do you feel about some light bondage? Haha"

"Light bondage sounds fascinating ;-)," Steve writes. "Or, we could go more extreme if you so desire . . . it's your call, as I am willing to try anything, (and you know I will respect limits and what not) . . . Hmmm, I may still have handcuffs somewhere (they are trick handcuffs, so no worries about losing a key, lol), and still have an eye mask, (intended for sleeping, but whatever!). I'll be sure to bring them."

The next day, on Sunday, February 3, 2008, Steve decides to commit mass murder. He's been off his Prozac for almost a week, and there's an important event in the local news. The day before, at Lane Bryant, a clothing store in suburban Chicago, an armed robber, believed to be a black man, shot and killed five women execution-style in a botched robbery. With this event, Steve begins buying what he'll need, beginning with extra magazines for his Hi-Point .380 pistol, purchased online.

He has an email exchange that day with Kelly titled "Why can't Helen Keller have children?" Kelly answers the joke with: "Because she's dead, haha. My residents are scared of storms, so this could be an entertaining evening of terror . . . How was your weekend? email me back if you're not busy. :)"

"No, I'm too busy," Steve writes back. "Just plotting world domination and all. Did you hear about the 'man in black' at Lane Bryant? Crazy World! Tell them that the thunder is just Satan bowling. The bigger the pin count, the louder the thunder. Or something like that . . ."

I have to wonder what "pin count" really refers to. Steve seems taken by the idea of fame through a high pin count. Perhaps he also believes in his historical importance, or even believes he is teaching in some way, similar to how Jigsaw teaches.

Steve sent a quote to Mark on February 2, a famous quote from Hermann Goering, second in command of the Third Reich and Luftwaffe commander: "Naturally, the common people don't want war; neither in Russia nor in England nor in America, nor for that matter in

Germany. That is understood. But, after all, it is the leaders of the country who determine the policy, and it is always a simple matter to drag the people along, whether it is a democracy or a fascist dictatorship or a parliament or a communist dictatorship . . . voice or no voice, the people can always be brought to the bidding of their leaders. That is easy. All you have to do is to tell them they are being attacked, and denounce the pacifists for lack of patriotism and exposing the country to danger. It works the same way in any country."

"Scary how that philosophy still holds true today," Mark says, "but, again, you see his high level of thinking versus the average person."

"He'll go down in history, right?" Mark says about Steve. "I always wondered too, as weird as it sounds, not did it for people, but . . . We had a fascination with school shootings from the point of Cho, how he got away with thirty-two victims or whatever he did. And how he missed some victims and his gun locked and all that stuff, right? And how he had backups and stuff. So Steve was very well-versed in the methodology of how to successfully pull it off. So he knew to have the right weapons, what weapons wouldn't jam. We had conversations in the past—and this was brought up with the school shootings—if you're going to do a school shooting, why go to classrooms when you could do it in an auditorium, when you have more potential to get targets. So obviously he took that into consideration, too. An auditorium would be the best pick because people are going to be all in disarray and running all around and you're not going to be able to escape, for the most part . . . And he knew that. He knew he could get in from the back and set himself up, right, because you're not going to be able to carry a shotgun . . . [from the front]. He knew the right actions to take, the right methods. He obviously was smart enough to know that the police would be on hand within a few minutes. So he knew that he only had a few minutes to do as much damage and get rid of himself. Because he's not one to . . . he would never be one to be taken into custody. Just knowing his personality. And he wouldn't want to go down with the satisfaction of someone shooting him. So he'd rather take care of himself and get it done with.

"I feel that maybe it wasn't for recognition," Mark continues, "but maybe because he studied these people and saw what they did, and he knew that Cho had mental illness as a kid . . . I think that one of the Columbine kids was taking Prozac. Maybe he just saw some similarities in that. And he figures go out and show, you know? He could have just gone there on stage and killed himself and it would still have been tragic, and it would have been for everyone there, to see that and view that and live with that for the rest of their lives . . . Did he do it because me and him had a fascination with school shootings, the psychology of it, so he did it because he knew I'd hear about this? I'd be like . . . not for me, but I'm saying did he do it because he knew it would be out in the public? I don't know. I've been struggling with, uh, the reason. He did a leadership guide for me and wrote these responses: How do you define success in your life? 'Personally, I feel as though success is setting and achieving a legitimate and viable goal, without the aid of shortchanging oneself or inflicting harm onto others, be it directly or indirectly.' Interesting, right? What do you think the most important things are in achieving such success? 'I feel as though maintaining a moral compass and a sense of ethical conduct is paramount in achieving any degree of success.' Interesting, huh?

"I did hear a story from one person who was sitting in front, stage right, in the front row, and when Steve started shooting, he went under the chairs and crawled underneath from the front to the back, and he could see Steve walking, like he could see his shoes walking by. So he's crawling, against the wall more, and Steve's looking for people. And then obviously people witnessed him doing himself.

"He controlled how long he was going to do this for, he controlled the room, for the most part, right, he controlled everyone in the room, and then he controlled his ultimate destiny, the destiny of himself. If you look at it that way, philosophically, it's about controlling yourself and controlling your destination because you weren't happy."

It's very odd to sit with Mark, Steve's best friend, and talk about all this. Odd mostly because he's so detached. No sign of emotion, just "curious about what went on in the mind of Cho," now applied to Steve.

He also still believes in Steve's goodness, as do many of Steve's friends and professors. Mark works in a corporate headquarters, and this seems a perfect place for someone with his interests to hide. He can remain completely anonymous. I sit with him for over three hours, taping our conversation, and we have months of emails and phone calls, but I still don't know any details about his personal life.

Kelly answers Steve's Lane Bryant email on February 3 with, "Nope, i didn't hear of any man in black . . . fill me in on the gruesome details! im going to tell the residents that the thunder is because jesus is angry, and probably because of something they did. world domination is what i work on in my free time as well. id even take a lower form of domination so long as i could kill people with no ramifications. but thats just me."

The next day, Monday, February 4, is the day they've planned for sex and bondage, but after all the build, Steve feels sick. "Hey, I'm not feeling so well and just took some Tylenol PM, as I think I may have caught a cold. I'm sorry to cancel last minute, but the last thing I want is to get someone else sick." Perhaps Steve is having stomach trouble as well. Stress and anxiety have always given him bowel problems, and he's decided now to commit mass murder and suicide, so that must have an effect. He responds to Kelly's "i hate contemporary theory more than i hate Mexicans . . . and thats a lot" email with "I rarely get sick, but when I do, it's usually pretty bad. I'll spare you all of the wonderful details!"

He buys from Bounty Hunter and Top Gun Supply, and he writes a check to himself for $3000 cash, then changes it to $3001. He also buys a spring-assisted knife. The next day, February 5, he keeps buying. Two nine-millimeter magazines and holsters from Able Ammo. He pays extra shipping costs for second-day air and goes to a Marilyn Manson concert that night with Jessica. On the way there, he asks her, "What do you think happens when we die?"

He describes the Manson concert in an email to Kelly on February 11, three days before the shooting. He's been planning mass murder for at least eight days at this point, but he's still chatty. "By the way, did I mention that Manson was AMAZING live. Probably the best part was him burning a bible on stage. On a hilarious side note, some of the audience members were Neo-Nazi party members and held up a 3rd Reich (Nazi) flag throughout most of the concert. The minimum wage black security guards and illegal aliens (the security at the Aragon Ballroom is outsourced/privately contracted out) were not happy about this, but the guys told the security to fuck off. It was quite entertaining. Seriously, though, the antichrist superstar logo kind of resembles a swastika. Well, be sure to keep in touch, and don't forget about me."

Mark knew about the Manson concert, also, "but again, that was something I didn't tell the cops, because they would blame it on Marilyn Manson. Steve respected Manson as well. He asked me to go, and in hindsight I should have gone, but he sent me this email: 'I went to his concert on Feb 5th, in Chicago . . . I've always wanted to see Manson live. I've always enjoyed his music, because beyond the initial shock value, all of Manson's music is a criticism of contemporary politics, religion, and especially media in some way. If you ever get a chance, check out his autobiography. Jessica has it, and it's very engrossing. A lot of his views make sense, but we are obviously obfuscated by his media image. Many casual observers don't realize that most of his music is a euphemism for broader issues. Example: the song Dope Show has nothing to do with drugs at all but rather the zombifying effect of media icons on our consciousness. Although that is precisely his point, he wants to be a hyper-ironic figure that knocks the hypocrisy of humanity.' When you see his writings, you can see that he just analyzed Manson probably the best I've ever seen it." And Manson is perfect for school shooters, because he confuses the concepts of suicide and murder: *Shoot myself to love you. If I loved myself, I would shoot you. What if suicide kills?*

JESSICA SAYS THEY HAD A BLAST AT MANSON. She didn't suspect anything was going on. But as Manson sings "Last Day On Earth," Steve knows this is coming soon. The next day, February 6, he goes to Tony's Guns and Ammo. He calls ahead, to make sure Tony will be open, and arrives a little after 5:00 p.m.

Steve looks at the display cases. He tells Tony, "I heard that a Glock is a good brand." In fact, his godfather, Richard Grafer, has warned him against buying a Glock, but Steve is interested anyway, specifically in the Glock 19, a nine millimeter. Is it because this is one of the two pistols Cho used, the one that did most of the killing?

Tony tells Steve it is a good brand, and tells him about the different models. He asks what Steve wants to use the gun for.

"Target practice," Steve says.

Tony offers to call the gun representative, who can answer any questions Steve might have about the Glock, and Steve says he'd like to do this. So Tony calls his dealer, Davidson's, and lets Steve talk with a rep. The only question Steve asks, though, is whether it's a good reliable gun.

Steve buys the Glock 19 for $554.60. This is the gun that will kill his five victims and himself. It's an Austrian military gun, light, perfectly engineered to kill people, its only function. He then asks Tony about shotguns, says he wants to shoot skeet.

So Tony shows him some skeet guns, tells police later that Steve buys a Sportsman Model 48. This is what Tony puts on all the forms, and he says he has to show Steve how to load the gun, tells police "it did not seem like Steven was knowledgeable about guns." But like other gun dealers, Tony is hiding things. Steve has traded in his old guns, for instance, and Tony doesn't report this to police. He will end up having to voluntarily shut down his business before the police make him shut it down. I think it's possible he lies about the model of the shotgun, too, falsely records it as a Sportsman model. The first ATF reports, and all the witness reports, are consistent with a pump shotgun, the Remington 870 12-gauge shotgun that Steve was trained on at Rockville. He even took a written test detailing how to load it, and in Cole Hall he will be very fast at reloading. The Sportsman 48 isn't a pump. Later, the ATF will change their story to say it was the Sportsman. Is this to avoid having to talk about how all the gun forms could go through with the wrong model listed?

Whichever model of Remington 12-gauge shotgun it is, this will be the one he uses first in Cole Hall, for shock and awe, for theatrical effect, to create confusion and chaos. He knows he's going back to NIU. He makes a reservation for a Best Western Hotel in DeKalb. He takes a cash advance against his Bank of America VISA for $5,000. He buys a Gator GC Dread hard shell guitar case for the shotgun, requests next day delivery. He needs to plan everything carefully. No screw-ups like at Columbine. No bombs that don't go off.

He wants to have sex, but for some reason not with Kelly. He checks Craigslist, the Erotic Services section, for prostitutes, and he posts his own ad there, too.

Just before midnight, Wednesday, February 6, "Katie" responds. She responded to his ad back in September, too, but they never hooked up. She's the one with 44Ds and "cushin for the pushin," ten years older than him and looks "more like the woman next door." He's not letting her get away this time, so he tells her, "I don't mind donating or what not." He offers to drive out immediately, with hot coffee and roses. He can be there by 1:00 a.m.

She can't do it right now, though. Her ten-year-old son is at her house. He'll be with daddy for the weekend, so Friday night would work.

"I'm just really horny right now," Steve emails. He could drive over right now and they could cruise around the block. He'd offer something extra tonight.

"So you want me to blow you in the car? :)" she asks. "If you don't mind me asking, what do you think would be 'worth my while'?"

"I don't know the going rate," he writes back. He's careful not to actually break the law in writing, and he's frustrated, because he can't quite get this to happen for some reason. Why won't she just meet? They talk on the phone, but this is frustrating. She has a sexy voice, but she keeps putting him off.

He's tired for class the next day, Thursday February 7. He argues with Sandra Thompson, one of his classmates. He finds her annoying, and he tries to put her in her place for a few minutes, but the others take her side and tell him to shut up. He's not really focused, anyway. He feels paranoid again. They really are telling him to shut up, but he also has this sense of them all ganging up against him, and this is probably the paranoia. At his next class, in the evening, Sandra's there again, but this time he doesn't say anything. He doesn't participate at all. Why is he even here? None of it's going to matter after next week, after Valentine's Day. He's just going through the motions so that no one will suspect anything unusual.

He's pissed off and frustrated that he can't see Katie yet, so he finds "Megan," also in the Erotic Services section of Craigslist. They meet that night at the corner of Prospect and Bloomington in Champaign, just off the highway, the same crack and ho neighborhood where he met Heather in the fall. He hates places like this because they remind him of all the shitty places he lived in Chicago with Thresholds, but at least Megan shows up. She's with her friend "Elyse," who doesn't look bad, either. He'll have to give her a call afterward. Megan gets into his car, a white Honda, and they drive around for a while, then park behind a building near the Econo Lodge where he had sex with Heather. He and Megan have sex in the car, with Steve on top. She's nasty, but that's fine, and they're parked for about half an hour, then he drives her back to where Elyse is waiting.

The next day, Friday, February 8, he writes a check to himself for cash: $4,600, then changes that to $4,601. It might not track that way. He buys stamps for the packages he's planning. He talks with Katie and finally gets her address in Seymour, Illinois. He arrives that night wearing his dark stocking cap. She's lit candles. He's brought cash. He doesn't feel like talking. They have sex, and afterward, he tells her he's going out of town.

He calls Elyse afterward, after midnight, calls Megan at 2:48 a.m. Does he meet both of them for sex? Has he been with three women that night? Has he also been with Jessica?

On Sunday, February 10, four days before the shooting, Steve talks with his father on the phone. He talks with his godfather, also, makes plans for the next weekend. He'll visit. They'll play chess. But this is just a cover, a lie. He needs an alibi. He tells Jessica he's leaving tomorrow, Monday, to visit his godfather for the week, because his godfather's health is poor.

He meets again with Megan that night at Walgreen's. He drives behind a hotel and they do it in the car again. They're back and forth eighteen times on the phone that night, dirty talk, and Steve also calls Elyse, which Megan doesn't know about. Something about the secrecy is exciting. No one knows what he's up to. He's free to do whatever he wants, like Nietzsche's superman. Except that he feels like shit, hates himself, is ashamed, has diarrhea, has to check five times that the car door is locked. He wants to die. He can't sleep. Sends an email to Kelly, jokes "Hey, isn't it black history month, and shouldn't you be out celebrating? ;-) For my celebration, I'm watching Beverly Hills Cop 2 on Spike TV while I doze off."

In the morning, about 10:00 a.m., he tells Jessica not to go to work. "Just stay. Just hang out with me today."

"I have to go to work," she says. She doesn't know, and he can't tell her. If she knew this was the last time they'd be together, she'd stay.

"You can write a book about me someday," he says.

"Why would I want to write a book about you?" she asks.

"I can be your case study," he says.

And then she's gone. He'll never see her again. Does he cry? She was his confessor. At Thanksgiving, he showed her all his mental health records before destroying them, insisted she read them. He told her about Craigslist. There was a time when he wanted her to know everything, but not now.

In their apartment, he saws off the barrel of the shotgun with a hacksaw. The guitar case, the hacksaw, the two new pistols, the extra magazines and holsters—he's hidden these things from her. He duct-tapes half of the inside of the guitar case, black tape—a riddle the police will never figure out. He puts the Remington 12-gauge inside, loaded. Picks up the case and it's not too heavy. It's strong. It'll work fine. He leaves his old shotgun in the closet. It's for skeet or birds, not designed for killing people, not a pump.

He's bought longer ammo clips for the pistols. They hold thirty-three rounds each. He won't have to reload. But the problem is they're so long, he'll have to carry the pistols in his hands. He won't be able to use the holsters and hide everything under his coat. And he wants to use the shotgun first, to create confusion. And for theatrical effect. That's Mark's theory from their discussions about Columbine. "Personally, myself, I was very infatuated with Columbine," Mark says, "just because of the whole process of how people did it, how they pulled it off, all that stuff. It's more of a curiosity for me. Me and Steve have talked about it." The word "infatuated" is interesting in relation to a mass murder. Is killing people sexy? Do we fall in love with mass murderers?

Steve leaves the long clips, leaves a lot of the extra ammo, too. He's not going to have more than a couple minutes. After Virginia Tech, the police will come quickly. They're not going to fuck up like that again and let someone walk around from place to place for hours.

He makes his bed, crisp, walks out to the kitchen to check again that he's paid all of their bills ahead of time. He doesn't want to leave Jessica with any problems. He walks back to his room and gathers everything. Puts the pistols and ammo in a duffel bag.

Does he pause and look at the Billy the Puppet mask again? Or the small doll, or the framed poster above his bed? Does he think about what he's doing? Or does he just do it, using his OCD to move through the actions, checking everything three times?

He leaves in the afternoon, drives almost three hours to DeKalb, past farmland covered in snow, checks in to the Best Western Hotel at 6:44 p.m. Uses his Chase VISA and goes to his room, 134, then calls the front desk on his cell phone after five minutes and checks out ten minutes later, at 7:00 p.m. He drives to the Travelodge. Maybe the VISA was the problem. He shouldn't have used a credit card. He could be tracked.

The Travelodge has a big black tarp out front covering the empty pool. Some kind of construction nightmare with chain-link fence all around. The place is a dump. The manager, "Matt," is a pothead, red eyes, impaired, slow to understand, slow to speak. Steve pays cash for his room. No records.

Perhaps he grabs something to eat, paying cash again. Back in his room, he sends Kelly his email about the Manson concert. She's written, "For my Black History Month celebration I plan to get a bucket of extra crispy chicken and a 2 liter of strawberry soda and have an In Living Color marathon." So he starts off his email with "Don't forget the watermelon! Sorry to hear about your sucky day, but things will get better! Right now I'm watching MSNBC and listening to Coma White." This is her favorite Marilyn Manson song. He tells her he's going to close his email account because of spam, asks her to call him later.

He erases everything in his email account and closes it. Jessica tries to email him and it bounces, so she calls him. It's a short conversation, seven and a half minutes, at 9:56 p.m. "He told me how sorry he was for all the times he had hurt me and made me cry and that I should find someone better," Jessica tells Mark later. "No matter how many times I told him that I loved him and how great he was, he never thought he was good enough." Steve also tells her, "I'm sorry things did not turn out differently for us. Thank you for not holding anything against me. I appreciate what you have done for me. I love you." He never says "I love you," so she thinks this is odd. She thinks he's getting depressed.

Steve has a call waiting from Kelly, so he hangs up on Jessica and talks with Kelly for half an hour. He tells her it was a bad idea living with an ex-girlfriend, because Jessica gets jealous when he talks with other women. They talk about the Manson concert, and he wishes she could have been there, but it would have been uncomfortable because of Jessica. He tells her he talked with and visited his godfather. He doesn't tell her he's in DeKalb. She asks what he's doing for Valentine's Day, and he says he isn't going to be around. He also says he wishes he'd met her before things "got so fucked up."

Steve talks with Jessica several more times that night, until midnight, and then he can't sleep. His usual thing, lying awake from midnight to

3:00 a.m. He gets up and sends Kelly an email at 3:23 a.m., telling her to call if she wants to talk, because he's cancelling this email account, too.

The next day, Tuesday, February 12, he buys four books for Jessica on Amazon, all to help with her studies. He includes the gift message, "You are the best Jessica! You've done so much for me, and I truly do love you. You will make an excellent psychologist or social worker someday! Don't forget about me! Love, Steve."

He also buys her a phone and memory sticks for $426, a purse for $302, sterling silver peace earrings for $38, data cables and other accessories, CDs, and he wants to buy her an engagement ring, something she'll receive after the event. He wants to take care of her. He calls her in the afternoon, but she's at work.

He tries to reach Joe Russo and also his father. Jessica calls him back at 3:38 and they talk for a little over ten minutes. He asks her what ring size she is and 'what finger a woman wears her marriage ring on.' He tells her she'll be receiving a package in the mail from him. She can't open it until Valentine's Day or it won't make any sense.

Jessica thinks he's going to propose.

A COUPLE DAYS AFTER MY FATHER SHOT HIMSELF on the phone talking to my stepmother, saying "I love you but I'm not going to live without you," she received flowers from him. A romantic gift from the grave, the same as Jessica will receive. And how can anyone ever make sense of this kind of gift?

One of my former colleagues at FSU, Thomas Joiner, is an expert on suicide, and he maintains that suicide is not a selfish act. "That's not the way they're thinking," he says. They often believe their suicide will help the people they leave behind. My father, for instance, believed his insurance policies would help us, better than miring us in his financial problems with the IRS. We'd be better off in the end. Thomas Joiner's father committed suicide, too.

After twenty-eight years of suicide bereavement, I'm moving closer to Joiner's view. At first, suicide seemed like the most selfish act possible, and I felt rage and shame. Now I'm not so sure. But here's what my father did to my stepmother, here's how he was a monster.

Eleven months before my father's suicide, my stepmother lost her parents to a murder-suicide. Her parents had a big house on top of a hill, overlooking an entire valley in Lakeport, Northern California. A valley with pear orchards and hills all around. They had horses. They were well off from a successful pool and spa business. I spent a lot of time at that house, riding all-terrain vehicles and dirt bikes, swimming in the pool, learning to play backgammon, hunting and shooting. My stepmother's father had a gun collection, pistols and shotguns, in cases. A room with dark wood and velvet. Many of the guns rare.

My stepmother's mother felt bitter about her husband. He had cheated on her, was thinking of leaving her for another woman. Their years together were not what she had thought they were, her life a kind of lie. I remember her sitting in the kitchen on a stool, her little dog running around clicking its nails on the linoleum. She chain-smoked, had a raspy smoker's laugh. I was always a little scared of her.

One day she went to the gun collection and picked out a shotgun and a pistol. She shot him at close range with the shotgun, killing him, then killed herself with the pistol.

Killing him had not been the plan, though. She included a letter to him in her suicide notes: "I'm really sorry for your last miserable 15 years. I really didn't know. I really thought you loved me . . . Above all, Rollie, be happy because I'm taking your hell away. I've loved you more than you will ever know."

This was a small town, a small community, and for their five children, the shame was nearly unbearable, but they all stayed. They fought each other bitterly over the will, over the money.

My stepmother had already lost her daughter's father to a car accident. Then her parents' murder-suicide. She told my father, right near the end, "Don't do this to me, Jim."

But he did it. And he sent her flowers that she'd receive afterward. And to me, those flowers are the greatest cruelty. So although Jessica Baty has lied to me over and over, and should have seen warning signs, and is one of the most psychologically screwed up people I have ever met, buried deep in denial and still not able, really, to acknowledge Steve's victims, the people he killed and wounded, I will never stop feeling sorry for her. Can you imagine believing a proposal is coming on Valentine's Day, then finding out instead that he's a mass murderer?

THAT TUESDAY AFTERNOON, FEBRUARY 12, after Steve asks Jessica 'what finger a woman wears her marriage ring on,' he talks to his father for about fifteen minutes. He gets a call, also, from the Navy recruiter, Nole Scoville, and puts him off, says he's too busy to come in to the office. This is remarkable timing, a last chance to go another direction. Does he hesitate at all?

Steve orders Jessica a platinum ArtCarved Montclair six-millimeter ring for $1,435.50 from Amazon. That evening, he talks with Jessica again for eighteen minutes, then again for fourteen minutes, several calls for just a few minutes, and a longer one for twenty-one minutes at midnight. What do they say in these calls? There are limits to what Jessica will tell me. She hides as much as she can.

Steve talks with Mark that evening, too, and it's a normal conversation. "He was asking me about someone I dated down in Louisiana, and what it was like living out there and a different culture, and we talked about that for about twenty minutes, and about the PS3 [PlayStation3], and that was about it." Mark doesn't sense anything wrong with Steve, maybe a bit formal on the final goodbye, is all. Steve talks with Joe Russo, too, for sixteen minutes, and Joe doesn't think anything is wrong. The conversation ends as usual, with "talk to you later."

Has Steve gone out at all today, even for food? He has Red Bull and cigarettes, a bottle of lotion on the nightstand.

Kelly sends him an email, asking to get together: "This week was craptastic. The ice on my windshield was completely impermeable to scrapers and ice melt spray this morning, so I was 20 min late to class as well. On a positive note, I didn't slip and fall once today! :) What day did you say you weren't doing anything later this week? I forgot already. We should do something . . . karaoke, movie, whatever. I just need to get out of here for a bit. Anyway, I hope your day went well and I'll talk to you soon!"

He answers her the next morning, Wednesday, February 13: "I know what you mean about getting out once in a while, Kelly, lol." He's been in the Travelodge now for two days alone, waiting. "The snow and melted ice were a pain to deal with today, but at least you or I didn't fall! Friday may work, but I'll have to see what's going on. karaoke is always fun!" But he's not trying to get together with her. What about the prostitutes: Megan, Elyse, Katie? They're all a long drive south, but "Sheri," a woman with multiple arrests for prostitution, is closer, in Chicago. Does he see her? He has handcuffs on the nightstand beside his bed, which he's mentioned before with Kelly, for light bondage, so maybe someone does visit. Sheri tells police Steve "seemed weird," tried to get her to come to DeKalb, and even tried to arrange transportation for her. But she denies ever coming to DeKalb.

Steve goes to the post office and sends Jessica a package with the return address of Robert Paulson, 1074 Stevenson C, NIU, DeKalb, IL 60115, his old dorm address at NIU. He's asked Jessica recently whether she remembers who Robert Paulson is, and she remembers he's the one who dies in the movie *Fight Club*.

"In death, a member of Project Mayhem has a name: his name is Robert Paulson." Immortality and martyrdom. The protagonist in the movie teaches a victim the value of his life by threatening to kill him. Just like Jigsaw. He self-mutilates, pours lye on his own hand. He builds an army, in which all are "maggots," with no individual self or even a name allowed, until after they die, starting with Robert Paulson.

The first rule of Project Mayhem is "You do not ask questions," just like the army Steve served in, with no reference to right or wrong, and though the project seems radical and to the left, it's actually libertarian and to the right, erasing financial records and eliminating all tracking of the individual by the government or banks.

It's all about the individual in the end, and in this case, it's a split individual. The movie begins with a gun in the protagonist's mouth, held there by his alter ego, Tyler Durden. Tyler explains the genesis of this double self: "You were looking for a way to change your life. You could not do this on your own. I look like you wanna look, I fuck like you wanna fuck, I am smart and capable and, most importantly, I'm free in all the ways that you are not."

With all his checking behaviors, Steve is fundamentally not free. Tyler Durden's freedom must look good, and Tyler himself (Brad Pitt) looks good. The entire movie is a meditation on ambivalent male sexuality. Tyler splices bits of porn into family movies during his job as a projectionist, and the final shot is a long one of a nude male body with a prominent penis and dark pubic hair. It's the final image in *Fight Club*. Tyler Durden is a hyper-heterosexual male, who fucks like someone who wishes they weren't gay wishes they could fuck, loud sport sex with women, over and over, in hypervirility. And in order to have this alter ego, the protagonist must make one promise to his darker self, that he will never tell anyone about his darker self. Secret sex, secret shame.

By filling out the return address as Robert Paulson, Steve left a text, a way to be read. This is how I find him most unlikeable, his thoughtful planning of mass murder, including control of how he should be interpreted. He left Nietzsche's *The Anti-Christ* as another text, and also Orwell's *1984*. He even marked a specific passage for Jessica from *1984*, a romantic passage in which the characters, who have given up all other vestiges of individuality, watched over constantly by Big Brother, refuse, finally, to give up love:

O'Brien had turned himself a little in his chair so that he was facing Winston. He almost ignored Julia, seeming to take it for granted that Winston could speak for her. For a moment the lids flitted down over his eyes. He began asking his questions in a low, expressionless voice, as though this were a routine, a sort of catechism, most of whose answers were known to him already.

"You are prepared to give your lives?"

"Yes."

"You are prepared to commit murder?"

"Yes."

"To commit acts of sabotage which may cause the death of hundreds of innocent people?"

"Yes."

"To betray your country to foreign powers?"

"Yes."

"You are prepared to cheat, to forge, to blackmail, to corrupt the minds of children, to distribute habit forming drugs, to encourage prostitution, to disseminate venereal diseases, to do anything which is likely to cause demoralization and weaken the power of the Party?"

"Yes."

"If, for example, it would somehow serve our interests to throw sulfuric acid in a child's face are you prepared to do that?"

"Yes."

"You are prepared to lose your identity and live out the rest of your life as a waiter or a dock worker?"

"Yes."

"You are prepared to commit suicide, if and when we order you to do so?"

"Yes."

"You are prepared, the two of you, to separate and never see one another again?"

"No!" broke in Julia.

It appeared to Winston that a long time passed before he answered. For a moment he seemed even to have been deprived of the power of speech. His tongue worked soundlessly, forming the opening syllables first of one word, then of the other, over and over again. Until he had said it, he did not know which word he was going to say. "No," he said finally. "Never see one another again?"

Jessica tries to make sense of it all in her emails afterward to Mark. She tries to put together a narrative that makes all the connections. "He was totally OCD, locking the doors, checking things, making me read a paper six times before I would turn it in. No one but me knew that he was on meds. He was embarrassed about it, which I told him was ridiculous. He used to be a cutter when he was younger. He tried to kill himself like seven or eight times. He was having big problems with his sister. They weren't speaking, and she said some horrible things to him. He was also avoiding his father. It was really hard for him to let me read his mental health records, but he wanted me to know about his past. I told him a million times his past was his past and I'd never hold anything against him, but he thought it would haunt him forever. He thought that he was a burden to me and he thought I could do better, and he didn't understand why I loved him, after everything that we went through. He was so intelligent. JT and I have been analyzing *1984*, *Fight Club*, and *Nietzsche*. It makes a lot of sense."

Jim Thomas (JT) explains things a bit differently. "I'm not looking for explanation or causes but looking at a story and trying to cast it in some sense-making model." Jim's approach is from narrative sociology, and there's an odd remove to it. He says "I don't look for value, I look for an account of the outcomes." But this is similar, I suspect, to the social-scientific remove Steve had in understanding himself through the lenses of *Fight Club*, Orwell, and Nietzsche, and I suspect is part of why he was able to plan in advance and finally do something so inhuman and cold. In other words, I think we can see something related and close to Steve's internal thought processes going on now in how his mentor Jim is trying to put together the story. The police, according to Jim, are doing exactly the opposite. "What they're trying to look for is motive, genesis," Jim says. "They don't understand. They're looking for comfort and predictability."

Steve's last call to Jessica is just before midnight on February 13, wishing her Happy Valentine's Day, promising he'll see her tomorrow. "Good-bye, Jessica," he says.

He takes the SIM card out of his phone, the hard drive out of his laptop, and hides them where they will never be found.

VALENTINE'S DAY, FEBRUARY 14, 2008. I imagine Steve sitting on the end of his bed in the broken-down Travelodge. Smoking a Newport. Stale smell of old cigarettes, of all the lives that have passed through this room. I know he's dressed in black shoes, black pants, his black T-shirt with "Terrorist" in white letters above a red AK-47 assault rifle. Black stocking cap above dark eyes, narrow face. Small mouth, almost no chin. His eyebrows are plucked. He's shaved his pubic hair.

Across his lap, the Remington 12-gauge shotgun, the barrel sawed off. One hand on the stock, one on the barrel. He can't sit still, though. Always fidgeting.

Beside him, laid out carefully across the bedspread, all pointing the same way, three pistols. Glock 9 mm. Sig-Sauer .380. Hi-Point .380. He picks up the Glock, checks the clip, makes sure it's full. Checks it again. Checks it again. Threes have always spoken to him, shown him what to do. Three pistols. Three shells in the shotgun. He could take out the duck plug, make it five shells. But then it wouldn't be three.

The Glock doesn't seem real. Heavy, but looks like plastic, feels like plastic. A toy gun, almost.

He sets the pistol down. Picks up the next, and the next, checks each clip three times. Checks the extra clips. A bullet is so small, so heavy for its size.

Waiting. Takes another drink of Red Bull. Pushes up the sleeve on his right forearm, looks at his tattoo again, Jigsaw riding a tricycle through a pool of blood. Cut marks in the background.

He lays the shotgun in its guitar case. Closes the latches, tucks all three pistols into his holsters, along with extra clips in their pouches, everything hidden by his coat. Kenneth Cole. Not a trench coat exactly. Nicer. Checks himself in the mirror, walks to the door, then has to go back to check again, just to make sure. Always checking.

He turns right out of the motel lot, just a white Honda Civic, nothing you'd notice. Left on Carroll Ave. Left into the guest parking lot.

He parks a couple hundred feet from Cole Hall. A cold, overcast day. Snow. Listens to a CD the police will find in his stereo. He's titled it "Final CD." Waits for the last song, Manson's "Last Day On Earth."

Class will be over soon. He must know that. Has he hesitated? Has he sat there in his car listening to music and considered not going through with it? He's almost too late. A few more minutes, only a few more, and everyone will be gone. Does it occur to him that what he's about to do is not inevitable, even for a life like his, so perfectly shaped for mass murder?

One last song. *I know it's the last day on earth . . . say goodbye.* Then he gets out of the car, grabs the guitar case, puts on a small black backpack to make it look like he's carrying books for classes, and walks the short distance to the back of Cole Hall. It's all brick, and there's a walkway here between the two auditoriums. He's close to the door that will take him backstage. He drops the backpack, opens the guitar case, picks up the shotgun, checks his pistols.

Joe Peterson is at the end of a lecture on ocean sedimentology. A lot of his 160 students are missing because it's Valentine's Day and they just had a test two days before, on Tuesday. Students at the top of the auditorium are getting antsy. Behind them, students arriving early for the next class keep opening the doors and peeking in.

Joe clicks to the second-to-last slide. He glances at his cell phone on the podium, 3:04 p.m., and steps from his podium toward center stage to give the last part of his lecture.

The door behind the screen bursts open. Steve walks abruptly onto the stage. He stands for a moment just looking at the class.

Jerry Santoni, a sociology major with an emphasis in criminology, a member of ACA, the group Steve helped found, has a first thought that "this guy's lost," coming in the stage door. But then Steve raises the shotgun.

He fires into the front row of students. Chaos. Multiple students hit, everyone rising to run. Unnum Rahman hears the shot and feels something dripping on her face. She has a shotgun pellet in her forehead. Steve's using only birdshot. She gets up and runs. But some students still think it might be some kind of joke. Jamika Edwards, for instance, sitting in the fourth row. Even though she's very close, she thinks this can't be real. Confusion.

Jerry Santoni is near the back, so he sees only a puff of smoke and a bit of fire. Jeremy Smith, in the very back, starts running after the first shot and is the first one out the doors, the first to escape.

Joe Peterson takes a few steps back to a stage door like the one Steve entered. He pulls on the door, but it's locked. He pulls again and again, trying to open it as Steve fires his shotgun two more times into the students. Jamika says the second shot is fired high into the back rows. She runs with other students down the aisle but ducks into another seating area after just three rows and gets on the floor.

"How quiet it was between the shots is still haunting," Joe says.

"He's reloading!" someone yells. And now others are running.

The auditorium has three sections of seats separated by two aisles, and these aisles are the only way out, which means everyone has to bunch in together. Most of the students happen to be on the side of the classroom Steve is on, so he has a clear shot with many targets straight down the aisle. Some of the students crawl under the seats to avoid the aisle.

Jerry dives for the floor and hits his forehead, gets a concussion. But he doesn't even notice, and he's able to stay conscious. His glasses have fallen down, so he takes a moment to push them back up, then he runs out, but someone trips right in the door, and there's almost a pileup. The guy behind him is injured and bleeding. "I remember the blood drops hitting the snow and turning it red."

Jerry is planning to be a police officer, and he thinks fast enough to take an immediate right turn to get behind a wall, then he just keeps running, all the way to the student center. But he feels guilty already. From his pizza delivery job, he knows the girl who was sitting next to him, and he didn't help her get out of there. She's on the floor, hiding under someone's coat.

Joe is hiding behind his podium, up on stage with Steve. The stage is large, and he's at the other end. "I could hear the click of the plastic shotgun shells as he was reloading," Joe says. "I remember thinking, 'How the hell is he reloading so fast?'"

The first call to 911 comes in at 53 seconds after 3:04. Two seconds later, more calls, and officers Besler and Burke gather info, pinpoint the location and basic description of the shooter. It will take them more than a minute and a half to do this, though, until 34 seconds after 3:06, when they dispatch an officer to Cole Hall. A minute and a half is not a long time, but in a shooting, it's an eternity. The police aren't going to make the mistakes of Columbine or Virginia Tech. They're moving as fast as they can, and the first officer who arrives is supposed to immediately go in, without backup. But Steve knows this new plan, too, and has planned his shooting to take only a couple of minutes. So despite best intentions, the police aren't really responding to the event. It's not possible to respond to this event. They're going to respond to an aftermath.

Steve fires the shotgun three more times, shooting students in the back as they bunch up in the aisle, trying to escape. At this distance, the tiny bird shot pellets are spraying wide, hitting many with each shot, wounding and not killing. That eerie quiet again between each round.

"I had two thoughts during his second reloading," Joe says. "I remembered that girl at Columbine hiding under her desk who got shot at point blank range. I also thought, 'I just got married. I'm not going to do this to my wife.'

"So I took off. I jumped down from the stage and ran down the aisle, except there were students everywhere, so it was more like spider-walking, using my hands, too. I was keeping my eyes on him as I went. I knew not to turn my back on him. I was halfway up the aisle when he turned and looked right at me. He had just reloaded the shotgun, but he dropped it. I didn't see him reach for the Glock. It was so fast, he just suddenly had it, and he fired at me. There was no change of expression, not even excitement. It was like if you're repainting a room at home, painting the walls, and you realize you missed a few spots, it was that mechanical."

This is Steve's first of forty-eight shots with his pistols, after six with the shotgun.

"I felt something like a strong flick on my left shoulder. I was wearing three layers, so the bullet snagged. I felt something hot and round fall out of my sweater and hit my knuckle. I looked down and saw two white holes from my white shirt underneath my black sweater, and I touched it quick with my other hand. It felt hot, and the sweater was cauterized, felt like plastic. I just thought, 'I'm really lucky.' And I also thought, 'I'm going to get out of here.'"

Brian Karpes is Joe Peterson's teaching assistant, sitting in the front row, in front of Joe's podium. He remembers Joe trying to open that stage door. "He pulls on the door like three times, and it's locked. It was the most crushing feeling. Your only way out, and it's locked."

When Joe takes off running during the second reloading, Brian runs after him. "I ended up at the back of a large group, though, blocked, and I knew I'd be the first to get shot." Brian's a big guy. So he dives behind the podium, onto the stage, on his knees.

"I tried to peer around the podium to get a look at him, but the minute I saw him, he turned and saw me. He turned and fired, and he pulled the trigger of the Glock multiple times. He just kept shooting me. I got hit right in the head. It felt like getting hit with a bat. As I fell to the floor face-first, all I could think was, 'I got shot and I'm dead.' I hit the floor with my eyes closed and a ringing sound in my ear, and I thought this was literally the sound of my dying, going into the darkness."

Bullets that miss are exploding against the concrete and tearing up Brian's side with shrapnel.

"After a while, though, he moved on to others and I realized I was still breathing and not dead, and I realized I should just play dead."

Steve jumps off the stage. Dan Parmenter is sitting next to his girlfriend, Lauren DeBrauwere. Media will report later that he was visiting the class just to be with her on Valentine's Day, but he's actually enrolled. He's a jock, a good-looking guy. His family considers him their "miracle baby," because he was born with a heart defect and survived surgery as a toddler. He's in the front row, tries to shield Lauren, and Steve shoots him five times—twice in the head, twice in the back, once in the side—and kills him. Then Steve shoots Lauren, twice, in the abdomen and hip. One of the bullets travels up and narrowly misses her heart. Then Steve shoots the girl next to her. "It was almost like he went down a line," Lauren's father says.

Steve walks calmly up the aisle, shooting students with his pistols as he goes. Lieutenant Henert of the NIU police believes he used the Glock predominantly and tried one of the other pistols but had a problem with it.

"It would be quiet for a few moments," Brian says, "All I remember is just unbelievable quiet—then a few more shots. Every time he'd shoot, I'd jump, and every time I'd jolt like this, I was yelling to myself, 'You've gotta lay still.'"

It's only a couple minutes, but it seems to stretch on forever.

Ivan Gamez is hiding in the right side seating section with his friends Sara Crooke and Angela Brocato. When Steve gets to their aisle, though, he isn't looking at them. He's looking only at the center section of seats, shooting students who are lying on the floor.

Gina Jaquez is lying on the floor in the fourth or fifth row with her friend Cathy—Catalina Garcia—and classmate Maria Ruiz-Santana. She hears several students scream for Steve to stop shooting. But he keeps shooting. He walks up and down the aisle, works his way along the rows. He walks closer to her. She can see his shoes under the seats, only five or ten feet away.

He keeps shooting, a few rounds at a time. Five dead. Eighteen injured. Samantha Dehner is one of the last to be injured, shot in the right arm and leg. Gina Jaquez is still right there next to Steve, hiding, terrified.

Then Steve walks away, hops back onto the stage.

One more shot. Then silence. Gina waits. Waits a bit longer. Finally, she taps her friend Cathy on the back. "Let's go, Cathy!" she says. But then she sees blood on the floor near Cathy's hip, and Cathy isn't moving. She shakes her, and then she tries to get Maria off the ground. Tries to pick her up, but she won't move, either.

BRIAN KARPES FINALLY NOTICES it's been quiet for a long time, so he looks up and sees Steve lying near him on the stage. "He was in a half fetal position, his back to me. Instinctively, I pushed my glasses up, but there was blood smeared on them, and they were broken because the bullet that hit me in the head had hit the frame first. I was lying in a giant pool of my own blood. There was so much blood."

He sees Joe's cell phone lying on the ground and tries to call 911 but can't get through. "I walked up the aisle and one of the students was stumbling, holding onto the auditorium seats. He's got a hole in his chest and is bleeding. He's passing out, and I couldn't hold him up, because I was shot in my arm."

"I grabbed another cell phone from the aisle, and this time there was a busy signal, so I thought things would be okay, and when I exited the building, it was kind of neat in a way, all the police and firefighters running toward the building, everyone coming to help. I tried to tell them there was a shooter, but I found out I couldn't talk. I found out later that the left side of your brain is where your language lobes are, so I literally couldn't talk until the swelling went down on that side of my head."

Earlier, when Joe Peterson gets to the door, as the shooting is still going on, he thinks he isn't going to make it out because there's a mass of students. "But nobody was shoving," he says. "It was amazing."

Joe doesn't hear another shot after the one that hits him in the arm. He gets outside, slips and falls on ice, and runs over to the next building and yells at students to warn them.

"Is this a joke?" they keep asking him, but he tells them, "I've been shot and I'm bleeding."

"I ran down the hall screaming 'there's been a shooting in Cole Hall,'" Joe says. "I ended up in the anthropology building. I thought he might be going from building to building, like Cho." It's frightening to hide in a room, since the door keeps opening slowly as people go back and forth trying to find out what's happened. Joe is so freaked out that "at some point, I threw a phone and hid under a desk."

The girl Jerry Santoni feels guilty about hides under that coat on the floor until after the last shot. Jerry still feels terrible he didn't help her. "She dropped out of school afterward and is still having problems," he says. He's also haunted by seeing Brian walk out with blood all over his face.

According to NIU Professor Kristen Myers, nine students are so paralyzed with fear they remain not only through the entire shooting but through the triage as well.

The first on scene from NIU turns out to be Joseph McFarland, who works in Cole Hall for Tech Services. He hasn't heard any shots, but he's heard the fire alarm. He checks the other auditorium first, then sees a guitar case and enters the rear stage door to see Steve, "dead on stage with a pool of blood around his head." He sees a shotgun on his left side and a black handgun near his right side, spent shotgun shells and bullet casings scattered around. He tells police later that the auditorium was "pretty much cleared out" by the time he entered. He calls 911, and a few minutes later, the police arrive, so he leaves.

Alexandra Chapman, one of Steve's friends, arrives in the parking lot outside Cole Hall at 3:05 p.m., as the shootings are taking place. Steve tutored her as an undergrad, and now she's a grad student in sociology. She knows Dan Parmenter, also, from lacrosse. She doesn't get out of her car right away, because she's listening to an NPR segment. When she does finally get out, though, she notices that people are gathered outside of Cole and saying they've heard shots.

She sees the first police officers running across the small bridge in front of the hall with their guns drawn and sees Chief Grady running with his gun drawn, which really scares her, since she considers him "such a pacifist and all about decelerating a situation."

Then she thinks maybe it's dangerous to be standing outside Cole, so she goes to the sociology lab in DuSable Hall, where Steve tutored her. She and eight other grad students and three or four undergrads decide to lock themselves in. Someone has been seen bleeding in their building, wounded, and they think maybe the shooter is in their building now. The phones aren't working because of all the traffic, the Internet is slow, and they don't know what to do.

They've heard a lot of different rumors, not only that the shooter is going from building to building but also that there was a shootout with police, that the shooter is in custody, that he's been shot by police. But they don't know what to believe.

They also don't know what to do if someone knocks at the door. What if someone is trying to escape the shooter? They wait in fear, and though they feel guilty, they think about barricading the door with the big file cabinets. They have the lights turned off, hiding in the dark. If Steve were to call out from the other side of the door, though, they would let him in, because they all know and trust him.

Kishwaukee Memorial Hospital is a new, large facility where everyone will be taken for treatment. It's the only hospital in a thirty-mile radius, and not a Level I trauma center. Later they'll put together a PowerPoint presentation showing how they responded. Much of the info in the presentation will be inaccurate, though, including when the shooting started, who was shot first (they, like the media, think that Joe Peterson was shot first), and even when their own units first responded. Most of this is NIU Police Chief Don Grady's fault, since he won't release info, even to partner organizations, even months afterward. He doesn't release his official report until more than two years later, and it's full of errors and omissions. The PowerPoint slides say the scene was secure at 3:15 and EMTs were responding by then, but the police radio traffic logs show the scene declared clear three minutes later, with a repeated request for medical units to come ASAP. In the PowerPoint presentation, all responses are organized, but the radio log has one officer asking where to walk his victim to an ambulance, and he keeps repeating this request for almost five minutes, from 3:19:30 to 3:24. Chaos is what's happening, and numerous police, fire, and ambulance units are doing their best to sort it all out, but there's also infighting from the first moments between police units. Lt. Spangler of the DeKalb police is the head of the Area Task Force, and he should be given immediate control of the entire case, but Grady refuses to ask for help. There have been several years of bad blood between the NIU police and DeKalb police, who feel that Grady has isolated, shored up his own control, gotten rid of any at NIU who would oppose him, and refused joint training that would have helped in this situation.

Kishwaukee claims they transport the first patient at 3:26, about twenty minutes after the shooting, which began before 3:05 and ended before 3:08. They transport their last patient at 4:53, an hour and a half later. Their ED (emergency department) has fifteen beds, thirteen of which are in private rooms, two of which are in trauma bays. The private rooms are large and meant to be able to handle trauma, so the staff is able to improvise.

On that day, when the first call comes in, they already have nine patients, with acute influenza, pregnant hyperemesis, cephalgia, pharyngitis, fifth disease, ulnar fracture, and three other pediatric patients. They have two ED doctors on duty, with a third en route, seven nurses (one en route), two EMT's, and one clerk. They find they don't have to use their "call tree" to notify anyone because the entire town already knows. The first ambulance reports there will be two or three patients. The next reports eight. The next reports fifteen to twenty. They don't know whether the shooter is still at large, or whether there is more than one shooter, or whether this might be gang related, with possible retaliation at the hospital. They have to figure out where to put their current patients, how to organize their staff, and whether to lock down the facility for security. They decide to lock down at 3:20, establish an Incident Command. They don't have their first patient yet, but they give initial staff assignments, set up wireless phones, and even have a preset media plan. They're moving really quickly.

At 3:20, media helicopters are already in the air, but the hospital is having trouble getting enough helicopters for evacuation of seriously wounded victims. They're told that only Air Angels are flying, due to the weather, so they're trying to get more from Rockford Memorial Hospital. They're also talking to their sister hospital, Valley West Community Hospital.

By 3:30, they decide to use the second helicopter pad at the hospital and quickly remove the snow from it. At 3:38, half an hour after the shooting, their first patient arrives, with gunshot wounds to the head and left chest.

Back at NIU, when Joe Peterson is taken, finally, to the student center, he says, "Oh my God, is this all that's left?" Because only a few of his students are gathered. "There were books, bags, shoes, and blood everywhere."

Jerry Santoni is in a squad car, listening to the police radio. There's some confusion, because DeKalb isn't set up yet on the newer radio system, and the police think at first that there might be more shootings in the library. They dispatch officers to check it out. They also follow up on a report of a trail of blood that turns out to be only syrup.

There are still a lot of students and teachers hiding in various rooms in all the surrounding buildings, still afraid the shooter might be going from room to room. Alexandra and the other students in the sociology lab will wait for two and a half hours. They're finally able to reach the sociology office by a landline and are given the okay to go outside at 5:30 p.m.

By 3:45 at Kishwaukee, the rooms are jammed and family and friends are arriving, taken to the conference center in the lower level. The hospital has social workers, EAP (Employee Assistance Program) staff, and volunteers available immediately to talk to the families and also to help find out who the patients are. There are numerous problems with identification. But everyone is doing their best, an impressive response. Two radiologists are doing "wet reads" of the X-rays, for instance, so there's no time wasted calling back and forth to get radiology reports.

The X-rays are disturbing. One nurse will say later she's haunted by the "silhouette of bullets," all the round shotgun pellets and larger pistol bullets transposed on the bodies. One shows two bullets inside the victim's head. The X-rays look impossible to me, unaccountably brutal.

Phlebotomists are on hand to collect and label blood and send it to the lab via pneumatic tubes. And as everyone at the hospital works, NIU is also working. They schedule a media briefing for 5:30. They're putting updates on their website and have a campus alert system in place that was activated by 3:20, sending out warnings by email, telling students to stay in their rooms, telling everyone to stay away from campus, and cancelling all classes. At 4:10, they let everyone know that the immediate crisis is over. By 4:15 they've sent a crisis staff to the hospital to help students and families, and the chair of NIU student services is there to help identify students.

At 4:53, the last patient arrives at Kishwaukee. The dead have not been brought to the hospital yet, though, and the family of one of these students arrives at 5:30. They're met by a social worker. Steve's story has ended, but for everyone affected, the story is just beginning.

Not everything goes smoothly. Jerry Santoni, for instance, has left his keys and cell phone in Cole Hall, but he can't get them back, and no one will give him a ride. His head injury and concussion aren't considered severe enough. "I was told 'the late night ride service will start up in two hours.' I was also told, 'people have been shot—your keys can wait.'"

The shooting is so impossible and disturbing for the victims, none of them can remember it entirely clearly, even that day at the hospital as they're interviewed by police. Joe Peterson was on stage with Steve, for instance, and he remembers white and red on a black T-shirt, but he doesn't put together that the red graphic was of an assault rifle, and his mind transposes "Terrorist" to "Anarchy." He also tells police that he thinks at least ten shots were fired by the shotgun, and that the pistol was silver. He hasn't had time to lose memory. Rather, his mind changed things from the moment they happened, and this is true for everyone in the room.

"I was there and I can still barely imagine what it was like," Joe says. "It wasn't real."

"I remember it, but it's like it was a dream or something," Brian Karpes says.

Not one of the witnesses interviewed by police correctly identifies Steve's shirt. Several think he was wearing a hoodie (a sweatshirt with a hood), though most recognize that he was wearing a separate black stocking cap. The clearest description of Steve in the police interviews comes from Jamika Edwards, and I believe she remembers him most clearly because at first she thought it was just a joke. She wasn't as panicked initially, so she was able to see. But even her description is transposed, thinking he may have had red hair, for instance, picking up the red graphic on the T-shirt. She says "he had a 'stoned' look on his face" and "his clothing was typical of someone you would see on TV that would do this."

As Joe Peterson is being treated for the minor wound to his arm from that one pistol bullet, he feels tremendous survivor guilt. "I thought Brian was dead. I asked the hospital if Brian was okay but they told me, 'We can't release that information.' I didn't know for forty hours. We call Brian 'Superman' now, because the bullets just bounce off of him."

At 6:00 p.m., three hours after the shooting, the hospital makes contact with the DeKalb County coroner regarding the victims who have died in Cole Hall. This is the first time, really, that the hospital finds out what has happened. They've been responding and treating victims but without context. Within an hour after that, at 7:00, their emergency department operations return to "normal," according to their PowerPoint, including restocking supplies and cleaning. The immediate crisis has passed.

An hour later, the coroner and state police arrive at the hospital, and the hospital is still talking with families of victims until 11:00 p.m., including having to tell some families that their loved one has died. It's not until midnight that the dead bodies arrive. They're X-rayed, cleaned, and prepared for viewing. The PowerPoint slide asks, "Who is going to help with this?"

The next day, the focus is on the media, titled "Fast and Relentless" in the PowerPoint presentation. "Be prepared for the amount of media presence during a disaster." The hospital, after their experience, recommends prepared statements by only a few designated speakers: "Think before you speak."

The media is certainly invasive, insensitive, and sloppy, with almost no fact checking. "It was weird reading news reports that I was dead or Brian was dead," Joe says. "I read that my head was blown off. I still read that I was the first one shot, but I wasn't. I read I was chased around in the auditorium, but that wasn't true. Why didn't the media fact-check? I read that a student saw me on a gurney with half my face missing. My sister's watching the news hearing that the instructor was the first one killed. The media has the attitude of 'It's the truth now, and tomorrow the truth may be different.'"

"There were reports that the TA passed on in the night," Brian says. "My aunt and advisor both thought I was dead. And my aunt couldn't get through to my mom because of a dead cell phone, so for a day and a half, my aunt thought I was dead."

"The *Today Show* offered tickets to New York with Broadway tickets, etc., for my sister's whole family if she could get me to appear on the show the next day," Joe says.

The problem is that everyone wants to know who the shooter really was and how this could have happened. Especially since Steve was a Deans' Award winner, a top grad student, someone "revered" by faculty, students, and administration. That's why the media is so invasive. They know they're not getting the full story. Even the nurses working at Kishwaukee sneak up to look at Steve's body. We just want to know. Joe himself will become obsessed with the event. He'll look up everything on Columbine and Virginia Tech, days online, but at some point, he says, "I realized I can't do this anymore. And I went through all of that for nothing. I didn't learn anything."

What amazes Joe most is that more people weren't hurt. "Six with the shotgun and forty-eight with the pistols," he says. "And he hit less than thirty people. Thank God he was a piss-poor shot."

"WHEN THE SHOOTING HAPPENED," Mark says, "I called Steve around 4:00 that day, or 3:30, and I was like, 'I've been shot!' I left a message like that, because I thought there was just a school shooting. So I was laughing, 'I've been shot! Give me a call back.'"

This is their sense of humor, after all. "He had a shirt—well, you've seen the picture of the one shirt, the one with the American flag with the gun. I don't think it's a big deal, right? But the media posted it up, okay, here's the gunman. But he also had a shirt that I thought was funny that just said 'Terrorist' on it. That's all it was. So the joke was, you should show up with this at an airport and try and see what happens . . . He also had another shirt that was funny that had a picture of a rifleman—it was the whole JFK thing, right?—and it said 'I love a parade,' something like that. I thought it was the funniest shirt, and it was one of those things where he had that shirt and loved it but wouldn't wear it out because someone might take it the wrong way, right? That's unfortunately the state of affairs we're in."

Mark tries Steve again and again. Straight to voicemail each time.

At 10:00 that night, after details on the news make it seem that Steve is likely the shooter, he sends a text message to Jessica. "Is Steve okay?" Then a detective calls him at two in the morning, and Mark says, "Oh, it's Steve." There's no denying anymore what he already knows.

When Jessica arrives home that evening, police officers are waiting for her. They won't tell her what's wrong, and she isn't allowed to enter her apartment. Instead she's taken away in a patrol car. She starts to cry, asks if something has happened to Steve. She hasn't been able to reach him all day, and he didn't show up for their class at U of I. The police won't tell her anything, though. A long interview at the police station, and she consents to a search of her apartment, so after midnight it's back in the patrol car. "Did Steve kill himself?"

Yes, they tell her finally, and they search all of Steve's things, all of her things, their life together. In photos of the search, she stands despondent in the middle of their living room, wearing a white T-shirt with a red, long-sleeved shirt underneath. The police go through everything, take things from her, Valentine gifts from Steve. The gifts are still wrapped. She was saving them for when Steve would arrive, planning to spend Valentine's Day together. She opens them now in front of the police. And they don't tell her about the $3,250 in cash they take, another gift from Steve. They take his copy of Nietzsche's *The Anti-Christ*, other books and documents that might help her understand. They tell her they're going to take his car.

Her mother and brother arrive to help her. She escapes to a hotel room. But the media's already here, a news truck out front, everyone asking for warning signs.

A TV news team shows up at Alexandra Chapman's front door by 9:00 p.m. They ask if they can film her watching the news. She doesn't know yet that Steve was the shooter. They tell her it was Steve, garbling his last name, and then ask again if they can film her while she cries.

Josh Stone knows right away that it must have been Steve. "I used to joke that he could be a mass murderer, he was so uptight." In the evening, he starts getting calls from the press, and the *Chicago Tribune* and *Chicago Sun-Times* both drive out to his house, even though he's an hour from DeKalb.

Several news teams show up at Jim Thomas's house. He talks to Michael Tarm from the Associated Press, who seems "a cut above" the rest, and also agrees, finally, to do a short spot on CNN, shot from behind, not showing his face.

What the press don't know, though, is that none of these people at NIU know the full story. Steve hid his life from them. So the goose chase goes on, through the night and into the morning, the demand for warning signs that, for these people, mostly didn't exist.

Kelly knows things. She breaks down when she hears the news. She has to have psychiatric help, goes into the hospital but is out after about a day, according to DeKalb police. "She thought she was in trouble" because of her emails with Steve about wanting to commit mass murder.

In the early morning hours, Detective Redel calls Susan Kazmierczak, who's out of town. He tells her that Steve was killed in the incident at NIU. She says she knows about the incident from the news. She asks whether Steve was the shooter. Redel says yes, and now Susan breaks down. She can no longer speak. After all the years of fear, of hatred, it's finally happened. For her more than for any other person alive, what's happened can feel inevitable, her brother a demonic force out of control for at least fifteen years.

Detective Lekkas from the DeKalb police department calls the Polk County sheriff's office in Florida and asks them to notify and interview Steve's father, who lives in Lakeland. Sergeant Giampavolo and Detective Navarro from the sheriff's homicide unit knock on Bob Kazmierczak's door at 5:00 a.m.

"I know why you're here," Bob says. "I'm the one you're looking for." He leads them to a table in the kitchen. On the center island, they notice a Friday edition of the *Lakeland Ledger*, which features the NIU shooting on the front page.

Bob tells the detectives that he heard about the shooting on the news the day before and worried that his son might have been involved. His fear was confirmed when Susan called him. Jessica called, also, at 3:00 a.m.

He tells them that Steve was diagnosed as bipolar at a young age and that he didn't like taking his medications. He remembers that Steve said other students at NIU were "overprivileged" and "uppity" and looked down on him.

Bob reveals that Jessica told him she knew Steve was planning to get a hotel room near NIU in DeKalb. This doesn't match with what she told police in her own report, that she thought Steve was visiting his godfather. What else is Jessica hiding?

Bob is in denial about various aspects of his own history with Steve. He says Steve was "a bit upset" at first about Thresholds but then it did not bother him and he liked it there. He says Steve was never arrested and never acted out violently toward anyone. He doesn't mention any of the juvenile reports. The highest praise he can come up with is that his son "was a pretty good guy." He puts most of the blame on the death of Steve's mother. The detectives ask about guns, and he recalls that Steve and Jessica and Joe Russo visited the Saddle Creek Park Pistol Range at Thanksgiving with his neighbor and friend Joseph Lesek.

In the afternoon, Susan meets with Detectives Redel and Stewart in her living room, and she tells them everything. His troubled youth, their poisonous relationship, her hopes that maybe things could improve when he moved here to Champaign for grad school. She tells them she's surprised he didn't come to her house to kill her.

The media are outside, but Susan refuses to talk with them. She writes a statement, "For release ONLY IF PRESS CONTACTS MEMBERS OF OUR FAMILY." Does she believe there's a chance the press won't contact members of her family? The statement, on the front door of her house, reads, "Our heartfelt prayers and deepest sympathies are extended to the families, victims, and all other persons involved in the Northern Illinois University tragedy on February 14, 2008. This horrible tragedy has our family in a deeply saddened condition. In addition to the loss of those innocent lives, Steven was a member of our family and we are grieving his loss as well as the loss of life resulting from his actions. As a result of our family's extensive grief, we will not be making any additional statements to the news media. We respectfully request that the media honor our family's wishes and recognize our grief following this tragic event."

It's a notably modern statement, asserting the primacy of grief and the individual and the lack of culpability for what anyone else in the family has done. In other times and other cultures, their houses might have been torn down and their bodies ripped to pieces, but in our time they can demand privacy to grieve, and there can even be a righteous quality to this demand.

It's impossible not to feel bad for the family, though, especially when you think of all the hatred Susan had to endure from Steve over all those years. Bob, too, is such a tragic figure in his one TV appearance, coming to his door to try to fend off reporters, that I decided not to try to contact him. "Please," he says. "Leave me alone. I have no statement to make, and no comment. OK? I'd appreciate that. This is a very hard time for me. I'm a diabetic, and I don't want to be going through a relapse." According to newspaper reports, "he throws up his arms and weeps." And his arms do go up in an ancient and impossible attempt to capture the enormity of the loss, his voice breaking. He's living something as extreme as Greek tragedy, his life suddenly on stage. The chorus is outside and will remain there. Only death will end his part, and this will come in October, but eight months is a long time. Steve's mother, the most culpable in the tragedy—the one who loved horror movies, who feared her son and perhaps could be blamed for pumping him full of meds, keeping him at Thresholds, and returning him there each time he ran home, begging to be let in—was spared this.

There's a chance someone else was more culpable, an older male in the family or a family friend who sexually abused Steve when he was young, because most of Steve's problems and a few of his conversations with his friends point to this, but there's no solid evidence, and it's wrong even to suggest this against any individual without evidence, since an accusation in any sexual crime acts almost the same as a conviction. We may never know exactly why sexual shame drove Steve so mercilessly from at least as early as junior high until the very end. It's impossible to say, also, whether he targeted women, minorities, and jocks in the shootings. It seems he did, especially women, but it's hard to prove. It's hard to say, also, why exactly he chose Valentine's Day.

And I have to be careful. Some in my own family blamed my stepmother, for instance, for my father's suicide, because he wanted to be with her in the end, somehow felt "shafted" (his word) after he had been the one to cheat and break up two marriages. Blaming women for men's sexual shame and despair is inaccurate and dangerous.

Homosexuality shouldn't be blamed, either. Denial and shame were problems for Steve, but not his sexual orientation itself.

Culpability, blame, warning signs. The NIU sociology department and all who knew Steve are caught squarely and undeservedly in the crosshairs. By the afternoon of February 15 at NIU, the day after the shooting, there's already a strong culture of media distrust and silence developing. The department holds a large group counseling session with about forty people, guided by a therapist, and Kay Forest, the chair, tells everyone that she's not going to be talking to media. This generates a false police lead that she's telling students not to talk to police, but that gets sorted out.

The department has been hit hard. One of the students killed, Ryanne Mace, was a sociology major. Several injured, including Jerry Santoni, were in sociology. And most in the department knew Steve well, remember him fondly. "I don't want people to think of him as a monster," Alexandra Chapman says, and her sentiment is echoed by many others.

At this counseling session, they go three times around the circle, the first time saying how they met Steve and how they knew him, the second time how they're feeling now, and the third time what they want to take from this meeting. It's a really long meeting, three hours, and emotionally draining for Alexandra. "It was odd to see my professors crying."

Jerry Santoni is surprised to find out that the session for the victims of Cole Hall includes all who were enrolled in the oceanography course, not just those who were present for the shooting. But soon enough, he sees the reason for this. One of the girls who wasn't present finds out that the girls sitting in front and behind her were both killed, which means she likely would have been killed. Another girl who wasn't there for the shooting tells everyone, "My dad's in the army, and he was upset at me for not doing anything." She wasn't even there. She's tremendously upset now, crying. "And then my brother was making fun of me, because he's stationed in Iraq and I've seen more action than he did." Her family's response is just unbelievable, on a par with groups who will push afterward for legislation to allow students to carry handguns in the classroom. The gun dealer who sold to Cho and Steve will give a lecture at Virginia Tech supporting "student conceal carry" two months after the NIU shooting.

NIU gives a press briefing on February 15 with a range of speakers, including the FBI, ATF, state police, local DeKalb and Sycamore police and fire, campus officials, and NIU's own Police Chief Grady. But "dealing with the media" is what Grady says he finds most frustrating, and much of the NIU and DeKalb community will become frustrated with Grady simply because he won't release a report of what happened in Cole Hall for more than two years. "He's just sitting on it, apparently with a 'there's nothing else to be learned' attitude," Jim Thomas writes months later. "Grady has pissed off a lot of folks here by stonewalling the info. Grady is an ass for not releasing the report."

At a vigil that night, Friday, February 15, there are six crosses, for Steve and the five he killed. This is when Alexandra Chapman sees that someone has draped and stapled a black Columbine shirt over Steve's cross, so she tries to remove it, and then a TV camera crew spots her. "It's like we're not allowed to grieve because of what he did. The entire world met him that day, and they all hated him." The person she and others in sociology knew and loved is being erased. They don't yet know the tremendous gap between who they thought Steve was and who he really was, so nothing about the event or the world's response can quite make sense to them.

The vigil is a large one, with about two thousand people gathered in candlelight. Jesse Jackson speaks. "Jesse Jackson, he's one of those people that any time there's a tragedy, he has to show his face up for a public image," Mark says, "and Jesse Jackson went to one of the services. So I thought that was funny, that Steve would be laughing."

Barack Obama also shows up, but he doesn't speak. "I really liked that Obama showed up at the memorial service, quietly, and didn't speak," Joe Peterson says. "He didn't use it for his own political gain. I told him how much I appreciated his presence."

The Lutheran Campus Ministry is holding nightly candlelight vigils, also. Condolences are coming in from everyone, including President Bush, Governor Blagojevich, and numerous universities. Virginia

Tech, though, provides the most amazing support, with every one of its departments reaching out to sister departments at NIU. With the increasing frequency of school shootings in the United States, our outreach during the aftermath should just get better and better.

AT QUARTER TO MIDNIGHT ON FEBRUARY 15, the night of the vigil, Greg, one of Steve's undergrad friends from the NIU dorms, walks past the security checkpoint in the Grant North lobby on campus without showing his ID, and the access control worker, Joseph Puckett, challenges him.

"Go fuck yourself," Greg tells him. He's drunk. The confrontation escalates enough that Officer Jennifer Saam from the NIU police is dispatched to break it up.

Saam talks with Puckett privately in the lobby, and then Greg comes over and wants to tell his version. And he doesn't want to talk in a more private location. He wants to stay right here in the lobby. To Saam, Greg "appeared normal yet slightly teary-eyed," and she assumes the confrontation is just from "high tension" on campus after the shooting. She asks him whether he's okay, and he says no. He tells her he knew some of the victims in the shooting. He was at work when he saw on the news that Steve was the shooter, and he immediately threw up.

Greg tells Officer Saam that he looked up to Steve, changed his major to political science because of him. He says everyone called Kazmierczak "Strange Steve" in the dorm, but that to him, Steve felt imposing. "Even though he was listed as 5'9", it felt like he looked down his nose at me as if he was 6'1"." Steve was about 6'1", actually.

"I then realized that Greg might be an important witness for the shooting investigation," Officer Saam writes, "as he might have insight into Kazmierczak's mindset." Officer Saam is smart, and she gets Greg to talk. He tells her about the pig he watched his uncle slaughter with a dull axe, finished off with a sledgehammer. He confesses being beaten for shooting a pheasant with the wrong gun. And he agrees to meet with an investigator, as long as it's not someone from the NIU staff. "I have absolutely no respect for the NIU administration," he tells her. "Dr. Kelly Wessner can go fuck herself. Same as Brian Hemphill and especially that hall director of mine . . . you know who I mean [Stephanie Mungo]."

"Greg's passionate hatred of NIU's administration was alarming," Officer Saam writes. "I knew that our department had prior interactions with Greg for various alcohol incidents and an incident with Officer Brunner. Greg is well versed in his constitutional rights and is highly argumentative about campus policies/rules." He's served on a housing governance board and a subcommittee called Believing in Culture. He tells her, "I was railroaded out of the organization. They told me to get out or they would put me out. They accused me of being racist, but I only liked to keep my meetings short and sweet—people were not going to waste my time by making the same points over and over again." He tells her he doesn't trust anyone here.

Officer Saam takes Greg to the Grant North Substation to talk with an investigator, but he wants to talk more with her, tells her he feels he can trust her. He knows her husband, Major Del Saam, from training exercises in ROTC. Greg tells her he wanted to commission as an officer in the army and become an MP, but the military wouldn't let him continue in the ROTC because of asthma. "Greg is resentful and disgruntled about his failed dream, by his own admission," she writes.

Greg says that after ROTC he went to the funeral of one of his classmates killed in Iraq. He tells Officer Saam that the Westboro Baptist Church protested the funeral. This was the kind of protest Steve wrote about also, describing it as "a religious right nutcase campaign to protest military funerals; their intent being to tie military deaths in Iraq to acts of god due to the United States supporting homosexuality." Greg was arrested for disorderly conduct for his reaction to their protest. He knows there was a vigil this evening for the NIU victims, but he didn't go because he'd heard the same church would be there to protest. "Greg did not trust himself to maintain control should he be confronted by those protesters again."

Officer Saam is a great investigator. She writes, "It is important to note that Greg lives in the same residence hall (Grant D Tower) that the threatening graffiti was found in last semester in December." According to Joe Peterson, this graffiti referenced Virginia Tech, said the mistake was in having only one shooter, and had a second sentence against blacks, mentioning the student center. Mark raised the question of why not shoot blacks at the student center. And Greg, Mark, Steve, and Kelly were all racist. Is there any chance Steve might have mentioned something to Greg, something that Greg perhaps did not quite take seriously? Is that why he threw up when he found out the shooter was Steve? I have no evidence for this, though, and it seems unlikely. Steve seemed intent to act alone and keep everything secret. But you have to wonder. "Greg is intimately familiar with the security issues on the elevators in Grant Towers," Saam continues, "and could easily have accessed the Women's restroom on the 6th floor. Greg currently resides on the 4th floor." Officer Saam ends her report with a strong warning: "This information compounded all together, I am concerned about this student being able to manage his anger, frustration, and hatreds." This could have been written about Steve. "I hope that Greg will be sought out and interviewed before he exhibits violence, either related or unrelated, to our current crime." I haven't been able to find a follow-up interview with Greg in the police records, and I'm helping to hide him right now by not using his real name, just as I'm helping to hide Mark and Kelly and others. Our concerns about privacy mostly protect the guilty and implicated. I hope there was a follow-up with Greg, and I hope they're watching him still.

The next day, February 16, there's another big meeting in the sociology department for staff and faculty to be trained to respond to questions from undergrads. It's a grief management session of sorts, but it turns into an exhausting therapy session, with everyone talking again about how they feel.

The sociology grad students keep in constant contact from the beginning by email and phone and text and in person. They have lunch, trying to figure out how they're supposed to help their undergrads and really respond, and their waitress figures out what they're talking about. She starts asking them questions, which feels overwhelming, and they think, God, if we can't handle questions even from our waitress, what are we going to do?

This is when Josh Stone goes around trying to help everybody, trying to be there for Jessica and other friends, and ends up drinking a full bottle of hard liquor each night. He stops, finally, when he almost gives his two-and-a-half-year-old daughter the wrong medication. He and others in his family have histories of drinking problems, and he knows the warning signs.

On Sunday, February 17, three days after the shootings, Detective Wells calls Kelly. He's found her from phone records. She made a call to Steve about forty minutes before the shooting, left a voicemail telling him she'd been hired for a new job. She tells Wells that "she never noticed anything about him that seemed abnormal." I just have to repeat that. She tells Wells that "she never noticed anything about him that seemed abnormal."

Wells asks Kelly for all her email correspondence with Steve, and she struggles with this, holds back some of the emails. "This is all very hard for me to deal with anyway," she writes to Wells later that day, "and I just want what we had to remain separate from the mess that's being shown. Like I have said, our last conversation has replayed in my mind so many times to find that one thing I missed . . . I know that your work is trying to identify motive, but there is no 'why,' if you understand what I mean. No one event caused him to 'snap,' as the entire thing was apparently so carefully planned. Steve was a very intelligent and caring person who eventually just let his problems overwhelm him. I'm sorry that it came to such a tragic end, but the only one who knows the events that preceded 2.14.08 is him."

On the same day, Jessica agrees, finally, to an interview on CNN, because she wants to dispel rumors that Steve was abusive. She says he was a nice, normal guy. "No, no way, Steve would never do such a thing," she says about the shooting. Steve was sweet, a nearly perfect student, a winner of the Deans' Award. Her voice in grief is a baby voice, her open, pale midwestern face reveals only her sadness at this inexplicable event. She's wearing an orange U of I sweatshirt, holds a love note from Steve she received the day of the shooting, along with her other gifts. "He was probably the nicest, most caring person ever."

She says she was his girlfriend. They'd been dating for two years, and he had recently gone off his medication because it made him feel "like a zombie." "He was just under a lot of stress from school, and he didn't have a job, so he felt bad about that . . . he wasn't erratic, he wasn't psychotic, he wasn't delusional, he was Steve. He was normal." Jessica seals the story. Successful student, caring boyfriend, sweet young man snaps for no reason, this event an anomaly in his life.

The next day, Kelly writes to Detective Wells, "It's hard enough to deal with what happened, but then I have to hear the 'girlfriend' on cnn all the time. It's just that now I don't even know the truth. He was consistent from the first time we met that she was an ex, they were roommates, he cared about her a lot but had been encouraging her to date other people because he felt she was really possessive and jealous over him. Now I can't help but question everything and it's frustrating to not have the truth. I contacted her through myspace (I know I shouldn't have, but when I did, I still believed she was the 'roommate') and now I'm certain that I'm unwelcome at any services for him after our brief conversation."

Jessica is still trying to make sense of things herself. Even a month later, she writes to Mark, "I've decided that I have some questions that might seem odd. I want to know exactly where he shot himself. Is that bad? When I picture him, I see him shooting himself in the temple. Does that seem right? He doesn't seem like a gun in mouth person. Sorry if this is disturbing."

She was Steve's confessor, after all. He told her everything, and he told everyone else almost nothing. So it's strange for her now to know so little.

"So we said he's not a gun in the mouth type of person," Mark says. "He's just not. She thought that, and I felt the same way. Probably the temple."

The truth is that Steve put the gun in his mouth.

"I had to look up pictures of what people look like after shooting themselves like he did," Jessica writes. "I probably shouldn't have done that, because I've been having nightmares since I looked it up, but it just reaffirms my feeling that he was someone else that day. It wasn't really Steve."

"It's been almost three months," Jessica writes to me later, "and I still wait for Steven to come home. When I'm at home, watching television, I still turn to where he would be sitting, so that I can comment on something. When I've had a rough day at work, I start dialing his number so I can talk to him. Even though I'm in a new apartment, one that Steven never saw, it feels empty and not quite like home. There are pictures of him and us everywhere. I sleep in his shirts and I miss him so much. I didn't realize how complete he made me and how lonely my world is without him here.

"I'll always be grateful for the 2 years that I spent with Steven. Even though some times were extremely difficult, I feel so lucky that he was in my life. Steven had a profound influence on my life. If it weren't for Steven, I wouldn't be the person I am today. He touched every part of my heart and soul. I wish that everyone would be able to experience what Steven and I shared.

"I feel responsible because I didn't know what he was thinking and how he was feeling. There is nothing that I wouldn't have done for him. I wish he would have talked to me about what was going on in his head. I don't think Steven knew what his final actions would do to me. I think that Steven thought that all the things he sent to me would be enough to get me through the devastation he left behind.

"Some people were angry when I told them about the wedding ring Steven sent me. I don't think that Steven meant anything bad by it. The ring was Steven's way of telling me that if things were different, he would have married me and we would have been happy. I think the ring was his way of finally telling me that he wasn't afraid to commit. I know that Steven loved me even though he had a difficult time showing me all the time."

Jessica beats herself up about warning signs, and also about the last day she saw him, February 11, three days before the shooting.

"You can write a book about me someday," he told her that day.

"Why would I want to write a book about you?" she asked him.

"I can be your case study," he said.

On the way to the Marilyn Manson concert the week before, he asked her, "What do you think happens when you die?"

A few months earlier, he told her, "One day I might just disappear and you will never find me. Nobody will ever find me."

A few months before that, he told her, "If anything happens, don't tell anyone about me."

NIU PROFESSOR KRISTEN MYERS talks about the "forward, together forward" campaign here, which is from the school fight song and is posted on the door of nearly every business in DeKalb. She talks also about the "new normal" approach from the administration. It sounds like something out of Orwell's *1984*. "Everyone is supposed to move forward now as if nothing happened, because now is the 'new normal,'" Kristen says. "But I'm not willing to 'absorb' any more and move on in the 'new normal.'"

Kristen's angry now because she adored Steve as a student and helped recommend him. He went to parties at her house and met her kids. "If I had the money, I'd move away right now. I'd leave the country, I think. Maybe Canada or Mexico." She was in Panera with her daughter and suddenly felt she had to tell her what to do if a shooter came in the door. "When I had to talk to my daughter in Panera, that was it." She tells me that a young woman on the faculty carries a kind of pop-up Lexan shield now to every class, a contraption made for her by her husband. And Kristen's husband taught at Virginia Tech before coming to NIU. His father and grandfather committed suicide. There's a sense of doom.

Jerry Santoni is "ready and anxious to move on afterward in classes," so he's frustrated by the counseling sessions, some of which he feels become "just random gossip sessions." But he can't believe the oceanography course continues after the shooting. "The teacher [Joe Peterson] was pretty relentless, even for the final. I took the class only as an elective. The only policy change was that we'd have announced quizzes instead of pop quizzes. I thought he would react a lot more sympathetically."

Jerry is in a bathroom on campus a few days afterward, his first day back in school, and someone bangs against a towel dispenser, which makes a loud sound. "I seriously went through three seconds of 'Oh

God, What's happening!' I remember the echoing of the shotgun blasts."

"The students were the most inspiring thing," Joe Peterson says, talking about how they forged on and completed the class. Less than 10 of his 160 or so students dropped out. "I'm not a victim of this guy," he says. "I'm a survivor of him."

But the damage Steve did extends to thousands of people. The funerals for the five students he killed—Catalina Garcia, Ryanne Mace, Dan Parmenter, Gayle Dubowski, and Julianna Gehant—are held the week after, from February 18 to 20, "but there are really about forty thousand victims," Jim Thomas says. "This entire university and community." And one could extend that farther, too, of course. The vice principal at Steve's former high school in Elk Grove Village tells me they can't even hold a fire drill now, students are so spooked. The effort put into emergency response plans at universities across the country mirrors the Homeland Security effort, expensive and entirely incapable of responding to a swift attack.

Steve's godfather, Richard Grafer, is "sick to death of talking about Steven. I didn't know him. For fifteen years we had no contact. Now my own neighbors drive by and point at my house. I've shut down my entire life because of Steven. I can't go to a grocery store without people saying, hey, I saw you on TV, your godson killed a bunch of people."

Josh Stone hits a setback around Easter, when someone burns Steve's cross. There have been other attempts to take away or vandalize the sixth cross, but this one hits Josh hard, and he's struggling again.

"I understand it's tough for the people who knew him," Joe Peterson says. "It's true there aren't a lot of memorials to him. And I'm glad."

Three months after the shootings, Jessica still cries every time we talk. "I feel this need to protect him," she says. "He was such a private person." We were supposed to meet for dinner, but instead we're standing in a Barnes and Noble in Champaign, thumbing through books on the tables near the front door. Her friend Josh is with her again. He's her moral support each time we talk. He doesn't say anything, and I don't know anything about him.

She shows me her new tattoo, six stars on her left forearm. Steve's is red and black, NIU's colors, but I don't think she realizes these are also the colors of Jigsaw, Marilyn Manson, Nazis, and Steve's "Terrorist" T-shirt. She touches one of the other stars. "I don't know the other names yet," she says, and cries much harder. "I'm not ready yet for the other names, for what he did."

After the shootings, Jessica received all those painful and confusing gifts from Steve, including the platinum wedding band, and even *Fight Club* seems to have a message for her: "You shot yourself," the protagonist's girlfriend says at the end, and he answers her, "Yes. But I'm okay. Marla, look at me. Trust me. Everything's going to be fine. You met me at a very strange time in my life."

"I'm worried about who you're talking with," Jessica tells me, and she makes me name Julie, Rich, and Adam again, Steve's high school friends. "I talked with Susan," she says, "and she couldn't remember them." So I mention the "wiretap" arranged by Adam, the Tubes, and now she remembers the stories. "Oh no," she says.

But the worst two, for her, are sex with his dog and Craigslist. "You can't write about those," she says. "Steve was such a private person."

"I have to make sense of his life," I tell her. "And sexual shame is part of why he hated himself so much, which is part of why he was able to do this. If I leave out the secret summer of sex with Nicole, or all the people from Craigslist, he doesn't make any sense."

Jessica is crying again, and I feel terrible.

"I'm really sorry," I say. "I've never done this before, and I don't think I'm ever going to do it again." And this is true. This story has been grueling, and I have no desire to investigate anything like it ever again.

"On the way over here," she says, "I was freaking out about talking with you. I was asking Josh, why can't I just tell him what to write and what not to write?"

"I'm sorry," I say. "And we don't have to talk anymore. We can stop."

She takes me up on that offer. "I need to go home and cry," she says. Afterward, she posts on her Facebook page that "Jessica is thinking that if Steve knew the consequences of what he was doing, I think he would have thought twice," and by this I think she means not only the deaths and injuries and effect on her, but also the exposure, Steve's private past laid bare.

Steve's memorial service, with his family and friends, is not held until June 28. They have to wait that long, four and a half months. Jim Thomas isn't able to go, it turns out, which he finds terribly disappointing. He's just returned from California, has a touch of the flu, and finds out a second cat is diabetic and needs insulin shots twice a day, but the main problem is that something really scary is going on with one of his eyes, so he doesn't trust himself to drive on the expressway. "I wanted to be there, if for nothing else than to support Jess. Both bummed and guilt-laden, but there's really no way I could have made it."

Mark goes and says it's good to find some closure. "Obviously it was a tragedy," Mark says, "and in any kind of tragedy, you have to feel bad for the victims, but Steve himself was a victim. And a lot of people didn't identify that, and mental illness. Steve was a victim of himself. I don't see that it was really planned. I remember back in fall of 2006 that Steve enjoyed the guns and the shooting range. In DeKalb, he went to the shooting range. He wasn't a gun nut, though. He owned a couple guns, but no big deal. The media, they'll put a spin on it and say he's a gun nut and then blame it on guns and all that stuff."

Jessica writes, "I don't think that the memorial helped me all that much. I just kept thinking how it was exactly not what Steven would have wanted. I keep forgetting that the memorial wasn't for Steven, but for everyone else. Jim was disappointed that he couldn't make it. I was devastated when he said that he couldn't come. There were a few NIU people there and that was comforting to me. Some UI people were there too, but they were there more for Susan than for Steven."

Memorials are important, and one issue still to be decided is the future of Cole Hall. The governor of Illinois and NIU's president proposed demolition, leaving the site as a memorial, and building a new "Memorial Hall" nearby for $40 million. But after more discussion and an online survey of students and faculty, the plan shifted to a remodeling for $7.7 million, no longer using it as a classroom, and building a new auditorium elsewhere. In January 2011, limited renovation work finally began.

Put into perspective, though, six gun deaths is nothing for the United States, and this discussion of Cole Hall misses the point, if I may be forgiven for saying such things. One weekend while I was in DeKalb investigating, April 19 to 20, 2008, there were thirty-six separate shootings in Chicago, with nine homicides. Is it "media spin" to mention this? Weapons included an AK-47 assault rifle, which is becoming more readily available in the United States. We average over ten thousand handgun deaths a year in this country, and the Supreme Court upheld, in June 2008, an individual's right to bear arms, striking down a gun ban in Washington, D.C., and threatening such bans in Chicago and elsewhere. After the NIU shootings, the Illinois state legislature tried to pass that bill that would have limited handgun purchases to one pistol per month per person, meaning anyone could still have gone out and bought a dozen handguns per year, and even that couldn't pass. DeKalb's own representative voted against it. Every time I drive into Champaign to interview Jessica, I see signs by the side of the road that claim "Guns Save Lives." If that's not spin, then what is spin?

I DON'T THINK I'LL EVER ENTIRELY UNDERSTAND the year after my father's suicide. I told everyone my father died of cancer, and I didn't see a therapist. I didn't have a real conversation with anyone. Instead, I shot things, the guns a terrible substitute. A year of the most basic brutality, a year I'm lucky to have escaped without hurting anyone. I was an insomniac—and would be for the next fifteen years—and as I lay wide awake in bed every night, I couldn't help thinking over and over about the .44 magnum my father had used to kill himself. I had fired it once, at maybe eleven or twelve years old, and though I had used both hands, it flew back so hard it nearly hit me in the face. But the scariest part was that it fired with only the slightest pressure on the trigger. It was difficult to put your finger on the trigger and not have it fire. So what I kept wondering was whether my father had really intended to kill himself. What if he was just thinking about it, just testing it, or what if he had one moment of deciding but it was only a brief moment and, with the hair trigger, that was enough? I wanted to hold that pistol in my own hands, feel the possibility, feel the heft of it and know what it felt like pressed against my head. And I'm glad now I didn't have that opportunity.

I finally sold my father's other guns when I was in graduate school. I needed the money, but I also just didn't want them in my life anymore. What I really wanted was for them never to have existed. But once I sold them, I was surprised by this terrible feeling that I had sold off a part of my father, because I have so little of him left. He vanished with his suicide. We sold our land, also, that hunting ranch, for peanuts, stupidly, and it was mostly the land that held our family's history and that connected all of us every year, scattered now.

I still love my father, even twenty-nine years after his suicide. The feeling hasn't diminished at all, hasn't faded over time, but I have nothing left to attach it to. If I could hold his .300 magnum now, would he come back to me, some closer memory, some echo of hiking with him through live oak and manzanita, watching him raise that rifle high over his head as we pushed through brush? If I remember that rifle, really focus on it, I can remember the sunlight on my father's light-brown curly hair, receding, his lopsided grin as he looked down at me. But more than that, I can almost remember how the moment felt, what it was like to be there with him, to hunt with him, what it was like to belong. My father was what attached me to the world.

It turns out I don't really have that many similarities with Steve. I certainly don't share his racism, libertarianism, love of horror, fascination with killers, military training, ambivalent sexuality and sprees online and with prostitutes, medication and mental health history, drug-dealer friends, tattoos, disturbing mother, interest in corrections, etc. But I did inherit all my father's guns at thirteen, when I was most hyped up on hormones, and the world meant nothing to me after he put that pistol to his head. I had nothing to lose. And I had witnessed a lot of brutality.

I watched my father gut shoot two deer once. It was on the upper glade of our ranch. We spotted a group of deer, including two bucks. We were so far away, they couldn't possibly sense us. My father sighted in with his .300 magnum. I watched through the binoculars.

A great boom like artillery, my father recoiling, and I saw the buck hit in the stomach, gut-shot. It fell over and began tumbling down the steep slope, gathering speed in the dry grass. It was screaming, just like a human being. The voice really the same.

The second boom and the second buck was hit the same way, terrible luck. My father would be upset. A gut shot spoils the meat. He was a very good marksman, so this was unheard of, that he would gut shoot two in a row. This buck fell and rolled the same as the other, screaming also.

The two of them tumbled together down that long glade as we watched, and I'll never forget their voices. I'll never be able to erase them, though I'd like to.

I think we can be damaged, and I think Steve's life was already destroyed before he left high school. He had an incredible drive, though, to make something of himself, and I think that must have made his final act all the more bitter to him.

ACKNOWLEDGMENTS

I owe enormous thanks to my editor Tyler Cabot at *Esquire*. He assigned this story to me, then worked tirelessly, every day, for months, through the entire grueling process of interviews, writing, editing, and fact-checking. The two of us were equally familiar with more than a thousand pages of information from the police files in addition to all the interviews, and it was an amazing conversation, the closest collaboration I'll ever have with anyone. This is his book as much as mine.

I also must thank Terry Noland at *Men's Journal*, who assigned an essay, "My Father's Guns," which became an important part of this book, and the National Endowment for the Arts for generous support while I was writing. The Association of Writers and Writing Programs has now plucked two of my books from oblivion and given them a life, so I can't say thank you enough to them, or to the contest judge, Lee Gutkind, and it's been wonderful to work with the University of Georgia Press, just as it was wonderful to work with the University of Massachusetts Press.

I greatly admire Jim Thomas for his generosity, intelligence, and strength to pursue the truth even when it's uncomfortable, and I was surprised that so many people would talk to me about such an upsetting story. Julie Creamer, Adam Holzer, and Rich Johnson, for instance, and many of Steve's friends at NIU, including Aimie Rucinski and Kathryn Chiplis, and another of his professors, Kristen Myers. This is a community of generous, smart, warm people dedicating their lives to helping others, and so it's terrible that this event happened to them.

Jessica and "Mark" will probably not be happy with some of the judgments and comments I've made, but I want to thank them for talking openly with me, and they certainly have my full sympathies in their bereavement, as do the members of Steve's family.

The book is dedicated to those traumatized by Steve's shooting, and I do believe that discovering and printing the full story is worthwhile. Joe Peterson and Brian Karpes, the teacher and teaching assistant in the classroom, have told me as much. They've said that not knowing was worse than knowing, even though the truth is ugly.